Manifested Action

Manifested Action

F**k Your Dreams, This is Reality

BIANCA MILLER-COLE
AND DR BYRON COLE

JOHN MURRAY

First published in Great Britain by John Murray One in 2025
An imprint of John Murray Press

2

Unless otherwise indicated, Scripture quotations are taken from the Holy Bible, New International Version® (Anglicised), NIV™ Copyright © 1979, 1984, 2011 by Biblica Inc. Published by Hodder & Stoughton Ltd. Used with permission. All rights reserved worldwide.

A CIP catalogue record for this title is available from the British Library

Hardback ISBN 978 1 399 80923 8
ebook ISBN 978 1 399 80924 5

Typeset by KnowledgeWorks Global Ltd.

Printed and bound in India by Manipal Technologies Limited

John Murray Press
Carmelite House
50 Victoria Embankment
London EC4Y 0DZ

John Murray One
Hachette Book Group
123 South Broad Street
Ste 2750
Philadelphia, PA 19109, USA

www.johnmurraypress.co.uk

John Murray Press, part of Hodder & Stoughton Limited
An Hachette UK company

The authorised representative in the EEA is Hachette Ireland, 8 Castlecourt Centre, Dublin 15, D15 XTP3, Ireland (email: info@hbgi.ie)

Contents

About the Authors

Dr Byron Cole

Dr Byron Cole is a multi-award-winning entrepreneur, mentor, investor and *Sunday Times* bestselling author. With a business portfolio spanning more than 21 ventures across the UK and UAE, Byron is recognised for turning complex business challenges into clear, scalable strategies.

He co-authored *Self Made*, *The Business Survival Kit* and *Rich Forever*, delivering practical and actionable insights to thousands of entrepreneurs and professionals. Byron is also co-founder of the Self Made Speaking Academy, where he trains individuals to package their expertise, master storytelling and generate income through high-impact speaking.

As a sales strategist and business growth specialist, he has helped clients and mentees generate millions in revenue. In recognition of his contributions to entrepreneurship, Byron was awarded an honorary doctorate by the University of Greenwich in 2022. He remains committed to helping the next generation of leaders build with confidence, clarity and commercial success.

Bianca Miller-Cole

Bianca Miller-Cole is an award-winning entrepreneur, *Sunday Times* bestselling author, global speaker and expert in personal branding and communication.

Rising to prominence as the runner-up on BBC's *The Apprentice* in 2014, Bianca has since built an influential personal brand. She is the founder of The Be Group, Self Made and Bianca Miller London, and has co-authored three bestselling books: *Self Made*, *The Business Survival Kit* and *Rich Forever* – each empowering readers to take control of their business, wellbeing and wealth journey.

As co-founder and chief storyteller at the Self Made Speaking Academy, Bianca helps individuals and leaders uncover their voices, craft their stories and become compelling speakers who drive both impact and income. She has mentored more than 1,000 professionals to scale their influence and brand visibility, and is a regular keynote speaker for global corporations.

Listed in the *Forbes* 30 Under 30 and recognised by LinkedIn as a Power Profile and Top Voice, Bianca continues to advocate for confidence, career visibility and legacy-building for the modern professional.

Acknowledgements

Thank you to Lewis Paris (www.lewisparisfitness.com) for his thought-provoking contributions and practical strategies to support us in living a long and healthy life. In a world where *biohacking for longevity* is more than a trend – it's a strategy for sustained vitality – your guidance reminds us that manifesting a great life means manifesting health, strength of mind and ownership of our physical future. Because what's success without the energy, clarity and resilience to enjoy it?

Bianca

To my husband, co-author, business partner and best friend, Byron – thank you. For the unwavering love, the late-night brainstorming, the shared visions and the courage to keep dreaming even bigger. Each of our four books has been a reflection of the journey we've taken together, and this one, perhaps more than any before, holds the essence of the life we've consciously manifested for ourselves and Ethan. What an incredible reality we've created – a life of purpose, love and legacy.

To our son, Ethan – thank you for bringing even more joy to an already joyful life. Who knew it could get better? It's busier, sometimes a little wild, but I wouldn't change a thing. You've given my dreams new meaning. Ethan – may you one day read this book, understand the love and intention behind every word, and feel empowered to manifest a future beyond even your wildest dreams.

To my mum – thank you for making this book possible in the most practical and profound way. For looking after your grandson so I could write uninterrupted, and for always being my quiet strength and cheerleader.

To our incredible team — you are the engine behind the scenes, the unsung heroes who support every launch, every project, every goal. Thank you for your commitment, your care and your belief in the vision.

And finally, to every person who supports the Self Made movement — from our clients and mentees to our friends and extended family — thank you. You are the living, breathing manifestation of the community we once dreamed of. Watching you grow, win and rise continues to be one of the greatest privileges of our lives.

With love,
Bianca

Byron

First and foremost, we give thanks to God, the ultimate source of our strength, clarity and purpose. Without divine guidance, none of this would be possible.

To my incredible business partner, soulmate and wife, Bianca — thank you for walking every step of this journey with me. This is book number four, and every word we write together is a reflection of our shared vision, resilience and commitment to growth.

This book, rooted in the power of mindset and manifested action, holds a deeper meaning than ever before. It marks a new chapter in our lives, not just professionally, but personally. The arrival of our beautiful son, Ethan, has shifted everything. This book is dedicated to him. Our daily actions, the energy we put into the world, the legacy we're building: it all starts with thought, with belief, with mindset. Ethan, may you always know the power of your thoughts and the value of taking bold, intentional action.

To our *Self Made* and *Rich Forever* communities — thank you for keeping us sharp, focused and inspired. You demand excellence from yourselves and, in turn, from us. Iron sharpens iron, and your hunger, passion and commitment to growth fuel ours. Every time we speak, teach or write, it's with you in mind.

A special thank you to our team. While your names may not always be front and centre, your efforts never go unnoticed. Behind every launch, every campaign and every published word is a team working tirelessly to make it happen. Your dedication allows us to focus on our purpose, and we're deeply grateful for that.

This book is more than pages and print – it's a movement, a mindset, a mission.

Thank you for being a part of it.

With gratitude,
Dr Byron Cole

Foreword

When I read *Manifested Action*, my first thought was: *you guys have done it again*. You've created something practical, digestible and most importantly, impactful. This book is refreshingly free of fluff – no complex jargon, no lofty theories – just straight-talking, actionable insight that speaks directly to the person who's ready to move. It's a guide that meets you wherever you are in your journey, whether you're just starting out or deep into building something meaningful.

What makes this book powerful is how it manages to tackle three areas that are critical to growth – and it does so with clarity and credibility. First, the conversation around manifestation is real. It's not airy or abstract. It's about learning to visualise your future so vividly, so consistently, that your daily habits and decisions start aligning with that vision. That mindset work – the inner clarity and control – is something I recognise in many of the world's top performers. And it's something I practise myself. You've shown that manifestation isn't magic. It's discipline.

Then there's the truth about proximity and networks. I've seen it over and over again – in my career, in the careers I've helped shape and in those I most admire. No one gets there alone. We grow by being around the right people. This book challenges readers to build better relationships, seek out smarter rooms and understand the power of access and association.

And finally, you drive home the single most important principle: action. Because the difference between ambition and achievement is movement. So many of us already know what to do – we've done the courses, we've read the books. But the gap between knowing and doing is where dreams often die. *Manifested Action* bridges that gap. It reminds us that without commitment, there is no progress. Without motion, there is no manifestation.

This is a book that will help you think better, move smarter and align your vision with your voice and your value. It's a practical tool that anyone – regardless of background, industry or ambition – can pick up and take something from. It's not about perfection. It's about progression. And that's what makes it so powerful.

Thank you, Byron and Bianca, for once again creating something that doesn't just inspire – it equips. It sharpens. And it serves.

Dean Forbes
CEO, Forterro

Introduction
Manifesting, Meeting and Moving

Welcome to *Manifested Action*.

Whether this is the first time you're holding one of our books, or you've followed our journey since *Self Made*, *The Business Survival Kit* or *Rich Forever*, I want to thank you – deeply – for being here.

Perhaps you were introduced to us through one of our live events, a corporate session, a mentoring programme or a course; perhaps it was through hearing me speak or working with Byron as your mentor or strategist, or finding yourself on the receiving end of one of my LinkedIn pieces or Instagram posts about purpose, personal branding and clarity. Or maybe someone just handed you this book and said, 'You need this in your life', and this is your first experience of who we are and what we do.

Whatever the route – you've arrived at the right moment. Because the truth is, most people don't even make it this far.

Most people *stay* where they are.

Thinking, wishing, hoping.

But rarely truly doing.

And that's why this book exists.

Who we are and why we wrote this book

Let us introduce (or reintroduce) ourselves. We are Bianca Miller-Cole and Dr Byron Cole – partners in business, in life, and now in parenting, too. Over the past decade and a half, we've mentored thousands of people – from aspiring business owners and ambitious professionals to creatives, executives and visionaries. We've sold tens of thousands of books, built businesses from the ground up, trained global organisations and stood on some of the biggest stages in the world. We've worked with a range of people on the cusp of something they can't quite define – but deeply desire.

Most importantly, we have created a community of changemakers who believe, like we do, that **your success should never be left to chance**.

But more than that – this book is personal.

This book is a first for us.

It's the first we've written since becoming parents.

And nothing reframes the concept of time, vision and intention quite like bringing a child into the world. Suddenly, the idea of legacy becomes real. The idea of prioritisation becomes urgent. And the idea of balance becomes . . . let's say *creative*.

This book was written while feeding a newborn. While prepping for keynote talks. While juggling travel, consulting, leadership, family life, mentoring sessions, baby sensory classes . . . and still somehow (miraculously) managing to keep our humour and sanity intact.

It's the first book we've written while living across borders.

And it's the first we've written with *this* level of clarity – about what really creates lasting change.

It's not just a book about manifestation. It's a book about **reality**. About building the life you want – without waiting for perfection. About being bold enough to dream – and brave enough to act.

Because we've learned something powerful: it's not just about the dream.

It's about the decision.
It's not just about belief.
It's about behaviour.

It's not just about what you want.
It's about what you do.

That's where *Manifested Action* comes in.

Why now? Why this?

There's been a lot of buzz around the word 'manifestation' over the last few years. You've seen it everywhere. It's on mugs, in memes and part of mantras all over social media: 'Manifest your dream life', 'Manifest your soulmate', 'Manifest millions'. It sounds exciting, doesn't it?

And in many ways, it *is*. We believe in the power of thought, belief, vision, intention. We've used all those things in our own lives. But let's be honest – the conversation has been hijacked. Somewhere along the line, manifestation started being marketed as this passive, airy-fairy idea that, if you just think hard enough, things will magically fall into your lap.

Like some kind of spiritual Deliveroo, people were told, 'If you think about it hard enough, it will happen.' As if the universe is just waiting to deliver your dreams by courier.

There it is. Manifested. Delivered. No sweat required.

Now, wouldn't that be lovely?

But that's not how it works.

We're here to tell you the truth: manifestation without action is wishful thinking.

Action without vision is directionless hustle. But when you combine clarity of vision with courageous movement . . .

That's when momentum is built. That's when lives change. That's where the magic happens.

Manifested Action is the bridge between dreaming and doing.

It's the reason we now live the life we once wrote down on paper.

It's the fuel behind every business we've built, every stage we've stood on, and every challenge we've bounced back from.

It's how we've created the lives we live now. Not perfect – but intentional. Aligned. Full of joy, challenges, meaning, movement and growth.

How to use this book

This isn't a 'read once and forget it' kind of book. It's a living guide –
something you'll come back to again and again as your life evolves.
Here's how to make it yours:

- **Each chapter is themed** around a key principle of manifested
  action – mindset, vision, fear, consistency, legacy and more.
- **You'll hear from both of us.** Some chapters are in
  Byron's voice, some in mine. We wanted this book to feel
  like a conversation – with you and between us.
- **At the end of each chapter, you'll find reflections
  and exercises.** Use them. Don't skip them. This is where
  the magic happens: in the quiet moments where you
  answer honestly.
- **You don't have to read it in order.** If you're dealing
  with doubt right now – jump to that chapter. If you're
  stuck in a cycle of procrastination – go to the chapter
  on taking consistent action. But if you *do* read it all the
  way through, you'll feel the full arc and build-up of what
  manifested action really looks like.
- **Revisit often.** Your goals will shift. Your circumstances will
  change. This book is here for every chapter of your life.

What you'll walk away with

By the end of this book, you'll have:

- a clearer vision of what you truly want – not just what
  looks good online
- a deep understanding of how manifestation actually works
  (and what it doesn't do)
- a framework for setting ambitious, meaningful stretch goals
- real tools to move through fear, doubt and comparison
- insights on how to sustain consistent action, even when life
  gets chaotic

- a renewed sense of confidence in your ability to make something happen
- an understanding of the difference between passive dreaming and manifested action
- a goal-setting framework that makes sense for your life – not someone else's
- the knowledge of how to reframe fear and doubt into fuel for movement
- the ability to take consistent, aligned action – without burning out
- tools to build a support system that moves with you, not against you

. . . and, perhaps most importantly, you will have gained a belief that your vision is valid, possible, and *waiting for you to catch up to it*.

You'll also learn how to live and lead with intention across our Five Principles: Career. Entrepreneurship. Family and relationships. Self. Health.

Because real success is never one-dimensional.

This isn't the end. It's a beginning

If you picked up this book looking for motivation – you'll find it. If you picked it up looking for strategy – you'll find that, too. But what you do with those things . . . is entirely up to you.

I (Bianca) always say: clarity is your compass. And now that you're holding this book – you've found yours.

The next chapter is yours . . .

Here's what we want you to hear before you begin:

- You don't need to be perfect.
- You don't need to wait for permission.
- You just need to begin.
- So start here.
- Start with belief.
- Start with bravery.
- And start with action.

We're honoured to walk this path with you.
So, let's begin. Welcome to the movement.

Bianca and Byron

CHAPTER ONE
What is Manifested Action?

Manifestation

Before we get to the action, let's talk about the part that's got everyone whispering affirmations and chanting mantras in their bedrooms: manifestation.

At its core, manifestation is the idea that, by focusing your thoughts, energy and intention on a desired outcome, you can, somehow, bring that outcome into your reality. It's a concept that's become wildly popular in recent years – plastered across social media feeds, woven into wellness podcasts, and scribbled earnestly into vision boards worldwide. And, on the surface, it's easy to see why.

The idea is undeniably seductive. You mean to say that, if I think positively, visualise success, and say it out loud to the universe, I can have the house, the car, the dream job, the love of my life and a six-figure business by Christmas? Where do I sign?

Manifestation speaks to a deeply human desire: the need for control in an unpredictable world. In times of uncertainty, it offers comfort. When traditional routes to success feel inaccessible or exhausting, it offers an alternative path. And when you're feeling stuck, it whispers: 'You can have more. You can be more. All you have to do is believe.' What a beautifully convenient concept.

But let's be honest, manifestation has also got a bit of a reputation. Somewhere along the line, it took a turn from empowering to a bit, well . . . *woo-woo*. You know the type of thing. The social media posts with pastel-toned quotes about 'abundance'; the carefully curated shots of someone meditating on a mountain top above a caption that reads, 'I aligned my chakras and the universe delivered a brand deal.' It all sounds lovely, but it's somewhat suspiciously light on actual *doing*.

It's this idea – that manifestation is simply thinking, wishing or dreamily staring into the void until the universe gifts you what you asked for – that's done it a disservice. It's been misinterpreted as a kind of metaphysical Amazon Prime. You order success with your thoughts, click 'next-day delivery', and sit back while the universe sorts the shipping. No hustle, no hardship – just thoughts becoming things, with a side of cucumber water and a scented candle.

If only it were that simple.

It's the *Isaac Newton version* of manifestation. You sit under a tree, dreaming about financial freedom or true love or moving to Bali to start a spiritual retreat-slash-coffee shop – and then, as if by divine cosmic scheduling, your dream falls out of the sky and bops you on the head like a metaphorical apple. Except, unlike Newton, you don't get the theory of gravity – you get 10,000 likes and a false sense of security.

Here's the thing: there is *value* in manifestation. Real value. The practice of visualising your goals, of speaking them into existence, and of believing in your own potential can have a profound psychological and emotional impact. Countless leaders, athletes, creatives and entrepreneurs credit some form of manifestation for helping them achieve clarity, confidence and drive. But that's just it – manifestation is a starting point, not a substitute for strategy.

Where many people get it wrong is in thinking that manifestation is *the whole journey*, when really, it's just the map. A very beautiful, often glitter-covered map, yes – but a map nonetheless. And a map won't take you anywhere if you're not prepared to walk the road, face the hills, and occasionally get your metaphorical boots muddy.

So where did all this come from?

Despite what Instagram might lead you to believe, manifestation is not new. The concept has ancient roots that stretch across continents and cultures. In Hermetic philosophy, originating in ancient Egypt and Greece, the idea that 'the all is mind' posits that reality begins in thought. Vedic traditions from India speak of *sankalpa* – a solemn vow or intention set by the heart and mind. Fast-forward to the 19th century and early 20th century, and the New Thought Movement brought thinkers like Phineas Parkhurst Quimby, Napoleon Hill (*Think and Grow Rich*) and Wallace Wattles (*The Science of Getting Rich*) to the forefront, teaching that focused thought could shape reality. More recently, *The Secret* (2006) by Rhonda Byrne mainstreamed the Law of Attraction, bringing manifestation into modern popular culture.

All these teachings share one core idea: your thoughts matter. What you focus on, you fuel. What you believe, you begin to build.

But even the originators of these philosophies never suggested that thought alone would be enough. They talked about belief as a foundation, not a finish line. They emphasised discipline, persistence and, above all, action. Somewhere along the way, the nuance got lost, and we were left with motivational soundbites and aesthetic Pinterest quotes instead of the messy, powerful truth: that manifesting is work. Not just *mental* work, but *real* work.

Manifested action: The missing link

So now that we've demystified manifestation – lifted the pastel veil and lovingly retired the notion that the universe is a vending machine for vibes – it's time to talk about the real engine behind your dreams: action.

This is the beating heart of everything we're going to explore in this book: manifested action. It's the beautiful, gritty, exhilarating intersection of belief and doing. It's the point where dreaming meets effort, where clarity becomes commitment, and where ideas become reality – not just because you wanted them to, but because you *worked* for them to.

Manifested action is the act of declaring what you want – and then lacing up your shoes and running towards it.

The idea sounds simple enough, but here's where people often stumble. They think they're taking action because they're *thinking about taking action*. Planning is not action. Research is not action (it's necessary, yes, but it's not the doing). Worrying? Definitely not action. And manifesting alone – well, we've covered that, haven't we?

Action is movement. It's decision followed by direction. It's the part where you roll up your sleeves and get involved in the messy, unfiltered middle of what it actually takes to achieve your goals.

Whether that goal is personal, professional, financial, emotional or physical, action is the key that turns manifestation into momentum.

What action really means

Let's strip away the fluff and say it plainly: you cannot think your way into success. You cannot dream your way into financial security. You cannot meditate your way into better health or a better relationship. You have to *do*. And that's not a punishment; it's a privilege. You have agency. You have power. But you must choose to use it.

Action looks different depending on what you want from life. Let's take a few examples.

'I want to lose weight.'

Brilliant. A powerful and personal goal. But here's what action looks like in this context:

- You *don't* just journal about your dream body and hope a six-pack materialises.
- You *do* start making choices: eating in a calorie deficit, choosing foods that nourish you, saying no when you want to say yes to your third Uber Eats of the week.
- You get up, get moving, go for that walk, hit the gym, do that home workout even when you'd rather be on the sofa. That's action. That's manifested action.

'I want financial freedom.'

Of course you do. Who doesn't? But, again, wanting isn't enough.

- You do the maths. You work out your current financial situation. You get painfully honest with your bank statements.
- You create a plan: saving, investing, building a side hustle, applying for that promotion, raising your rates, launching that product.
- You do the actual work that moves the needle. That's action.

'I want children.'

This one's big. Emotional. Deep. But, still, it requires *doing*.

- You prepare your body/bodies for natural conception, you take the supplements, you do the necessary. You have the hard conversations. You speak to medical professionals, explore IVF, or adoption, or surrogacy.
- You make the appointments, fill out the forms, get on the lists, show up for the scans, the treatments, the paperwork, the tears, the hope, the grind. That is action.

You see the pattern here. It doesn't matter what the goal is; if you want it, you must identify what it requires and commit to doing *that*. And yes, it will look different for every single one of us, depending on our circumstances, privileges, challenges and timing. But the principle is universal:

You cannot just want. You must *work out what is required*, and then do it.

That's what this book is about. Not just visualising your goals, but *realising* them. Not just whispering your dreams to the stars, but building a ladder and climbing towards them, rung by rung. Not just setting intentions, but aligning every part of your life – your habits, your energy, your environment, your time – to those intentions.

A goal without a plan is just a wish

We've all made wishes. Some of them fleeting, some of them fierce. But no matter how strong your wishing game is, you cannot build a life on wishes alone. You need a blueprint. You need a plan. And you need to act on it.

Manifested action is that plan in motion. It's your blueprint coming to life – sketched with belief and built with action.

Over the coming chapters, we'll break down exactly how to do that. We'll explore the mindset, the systems, the habits and the resilience required to go from *I want it* to *I have it*. Because here's the truth: the life you love isn't just something you imagine, it's something you create.

And it starts with this: understanding that wishing is lovely, but doing is everything.

Manifested action in motion

To truly understand the magic of manifested action, we must look at how it plays out in real life – when vision and belief are matched by unwavering effort. It's easy to talk about dreams; what separates the dreamers from the doers is what they're willing to put behind those dreams when no one else believes in them.

Take Serena Williams, for example. A global icon, a 23-time Grand Slam champion, and arguably the greatest tennis player in history. But Serena's legacy wasn't built on manifestation alone. She visualised greatness, yes, but what transformed that visualisation into a reality was the unrelenting grind that came behind it. And central to that journey was her father, Richard Williams.

The 2021 film *King Richard* gives us a powerful insight into the man who saw greatness in his daughters long before the world ever did. Richard didn't just believe Serena and Venus could dominate a sport historically steeped in wealth and exclusivity – he *decided* they would. He wrote a 78-page plan before they were even born. He taught himself the game, coached them on cracked public courts in Compton, California, and shielded them from burnout and exploitation. The Williams family didn't have the privilege, the resources or the racial profile typically associated with tennis royalty. But they had vision. And, crucially, they had action. Every single day.

Richard Williams didn't wait for permission. He didn't see the odds and retreat. He saw the goal and advanced. That's manifested action in its most relentless form: belief, backed by bold and consistent doing.

Now contrast that with another titan, this time in business: Sir Richard Branson. A visionary and a force of nature, yes, but also someone who's spent decades pairing imagination with bold execution. From launching a record label in a church crypt to founding airlines and even sending rockets into space, Branson has shown time and time again what's possible when you pair a big dream with even bigger action.

But here's what most people miss: Branson has failed – spectacularly. Virgin Cola, meant to rival Coca-Cola, fizzled out. Virgin Brides, Virgin Cars, Virgin Digital – all ambitious ventures that quietly folded. In the early days of Virgin Records, he came dangerously close to bankruptcy, even remortgaging his family home to keep things afloat. These weren't minor blips. They were full-blown setbacks. But he didn't pack it in.

He didn't say, 'Well, I tried to manifest something once, and it didn't work, so that's me done.' He analysed, adjusted and launched again. Again and again.

Because here's the truth: manifested action doesn't mean you'll get it right the first time. It means you keep showing up, keep doing, keep learning, even when the dream gets heavy and the plan goes off course.

Failure isn't the opposite of success – it's a critical part of it.

What sets people like Richard Williams and Richard Branson apart is not the size of their vision, it's the size of their action. They didn't just whisper their dreams to the universe and wait. They built. They risked. They endured. And when things didn't go to plan, they went again.

That's the heartbeat of this book.

It's not just about manifesting the life you want – it's about choosing it daily, working for it consistently, and getting back up if it doesn't happen the first time. Manifested action isn't about a one-off visionboard miracle. It's about the lifelong journey of aligning your thoughts, decisions, energy and effort to build the life you love.

Why manifestation alone is not enough

In our previous book, *The Business Survival Kit*, we spoke openly about the law of attraction – the idea that you attract into your life what you focus on most. While many readers resonated with that message, we also received some strong responses, particularly from people of faith. A few told us, quite candidly, 'You lost me at the law of attraction.' For them, the very mention of it felt like we were veering too far into spiritual fluff – into territory they felt was at odds with their beliefs.

But here's the thing: this concept isn't at odds with faith – it's embedded in it.

If you look closely, across many of the world's major religions, you'll find recurring themes: the power of thought, the necessity of action, the importance of hope, and the belief that we are here to create, build and grow with intention. What some call 'manifestation', others call prayer, faith or trust in divine purpose.

Let's start with the Bible. In Proverbs 23:7, we're told: 'For as he thinketh in his heart, so is he.'[1] That sounds remarkably like the law of attraction, doesn't it? Your thoughts shape your reality. Or how about Philippians 4:13: 'I can do all this through him who gives me strength.'[2] That's belief. That's empowerment. That's a mindset of possibility, grounded in faith.

And it's not just about belief, it's about what you do with it. In Proverbs 21:5, the message is clear: 'The plans of the diligent lead to profit as surely as haste leads to poverty.'[3] Planning. Hard work. Action. These are spiritual principles.

In Islam, you'll find verses like, 'Indeed, with hardship comes ease' (Surah Ash-Sharh 94:6), and, 'Do not despair of the mercy of Allah' (Surah Az-Zumar 39:53), which speak to maintaining hope and perseverance through trials.[4] You are not encouraged to sit idly and wait, you're called to have faith – to trust in divine timing, yes, but also to strive.

The Bhagavad Gita, central to Hindu philosophy, offers this line in Chapter 6, Verse 5: 'One must elevate oneself by one's own mind. The mind is the friend of the conditioned soul, and his enemy as well.'[5] In other words, how you think matters. Your mindset can lift you or limit you, and it's your responsibility to steward it wisely.

Whether you're Christian, Muslim, Hindu, spiritual but not religious, or completely non-religious, the principle is universal: what you believe, and what you do with that belief, shapes your life.

And yet, in today's world, the word 'manifestation' often gets misunderstood. For some, it conjures images of someone whispering to the moon and waiting for miracles to arrive in first-class packaging.

But this isn't about passivity disguised as spirituality. This is about clarity, commitment and consistent action.

If you're religious, you might believe you were created by a higher power for a purpose. If you're not, you might believe in the power of self-determination and resilience. Either way, we believe the message is the same: you were designed to create, to contribute, to move – and to *keep* moving.

Whether you call it divine design or personal drive, manifested action is about using what you've been given – your mind, your body, your voice, your gifts – to shape the life you want.

You can pray, meditate, visualise, journal – all of which are powerful practices – but none of them replace action. Faith without works is, as the Bible says, dead. And manifestation without movement is exactly the same.

You are here to build something. Something meaningful. Something abundant. That might mean building a business, a family, a legacy, a healthier body, or a stronger relationship with yourself. Whatever it is, it starts with belief, but it is built by action.

Manifested action in our lives: A personal reflection

As a married couple, we often find ourselves dancing between two worlds: our individual goals and our shared vision. Both matter. Both need space. And both need attention. So before we ever get to a spreadsheet or start building the action plan, we each start by doing what we call manifesting in our own lane – creating the vision in our minds of what that goal might look like when it becomes real. Then, and only then, do we come together to align on the dream, refine the details, and commit to the steps that will get us there.

Let's take you back to 2017.

At the time, we were living in our second home – a beautifully refurbished three-bedroom house. We'd purchased it with the intention of transforming it, and transform it we had – although the process wasn't without its surprises. On one visit we made to check in with the builder, we walked upstairs, only to discover that the wall between the bedroom and the bathroom had vanished entirely.

When we asked what had happened, he shrugged and said matter-of-factly, 'The wall was sh*t, so I took it down.' Lovely. And when we looked up? No ceiling. Just a view of the stars. Apparently, the roof wasn't doing too well, either.

But, in the end, after all the mess and madness, it became our home – a place full of memories and milestones. We were happy there. But as our businesses grew, as our lives expanded, so did our vision.

We both started manifesting separately, scribbling ideas and aspirations in notebooks, thinking about what came next. Bianca wanted a double-fronted home, with a driveway and gates. Byron had his eye on something bigger – a five-bedroom house with a swimming pool. We didn't know how or when, but we knew *what*.

And then we did what we always do – we brought those visions together and aligned. We compared notes. We talked numbers. We looked at our finances (over and over and over again), reviewed what we needed to do in business to bridge the gap, and began searching.

It took nearly a year of viewings, rejections, spreadsheets, awkward estate agent small talk, and moments of, 'Maybe we're dreaming too big.' But we held the vision. And we stayed in motion.

Eventually, we found it: a six-bedroom, double-fronted house on half an acre of land, with a gated driveway and, yes, a swimming pool. We'd manifested it. And then we'd taken the action needed to bring it to life.

Sounds neat and tidy, right? A picture-perfect success story. Except, of course, it wasn't.

What we bought was a doer-upper. And as anyone who has ever embarked on a renovation will tell you, that's code for: 'This might break you.' The builder took twice as long as planned, and the budget? Let's just say it didn't just stretch, it *snapped*. We poured time, energy, money (and, let's be honest, some tears) into that home. And yes, we ended up with the house we'd dreamed of, but we also ended up with debt, a few new grey hairs and a crash course in project management we'd never signed up for.

But, still, we did it. Because that's what manifested action looks like in the real world.

It's not just dreaming big and smiling at the moon. It's manifesting the goal, then grafting through the process. It's balancing belief with spreadsheets, hope with heavy lifting. It's setbacks, recalculations and resilience. It's late nights, deep sighs, and standing in the middle of a building site trying to remember why you even started.

But eventually, it's also walking into a home that once lived in your mind and now belongs to your reality.

That's what this book is about. Not perfect stories. Not magic. Not one-size-fits-all formulas. But the truth of manifested action: that, with belief and bravery, vision and movement, patience and persistence, you can build the life you want – one decision, one sacrifice and one bold step at a time.

The Five Principles of Manifested Action

So now that we've unpacked what manifestation really means, why action is essential, and how it shows up in our own lives and in the lives of people we admire, the next step is to give you a framework. Because here's the truth: success, however you define it, requires structure.

Manifested action isn't just a concept. It's a practice. And, like any meaningful practice, it needs principles – foundation blocks that can support your journey, whether you're dreaming of a career change, building a business, relocating your family or simply becoming the best version of yourself.

Throughout this book, we'll return again and again to what we call the five key principles of manifested action.

1 **Career** Whether you're climbing the corporate ladder, pivoting into a new industry, or simply trying to figure out what's next, your career is a huge part of how you spend your time and contribute to the world. Manifested action here means getting clear on the role you want, the lifestyle you crave, and the growth you seek – and then doing the work to position yourself accordingly.

Think: new qualifications, stronger networks, better boundaries, bolder applications.

2 **Entrepreneurship** For the business-builders, side-hustlers, creatives and visionaries: your dreams won't build themselves. From launch to legacy, manifested action in entrepreneurship is about clarity, consistency and courage. It's marketing the idea, testing the product, learning the numbers, facing the fear of failure – and going again anyway.

We'll talk about what it means to show up not just *in* your business but *for* your business.

3 **Family and relationships** This isn't just about romantic partnerships or parenting, it's about the people who shape your world. Manifested action in this principle is about intention and investment: creating space for connection, navigating transitions, setting healthy expectations, and building relationships that support the life you're working towards.

Because it's hard to thrive if your personal world is in chaos, or if the people you love feel left behind.

4 **Self** Your mindset. Your environment. Your confidence. Your energy. This principle is everything to do with who you are when no one's watching. Manifested action here is about how you take care of yourself, grow yourself and back yourself, especially when things don't go to plan.

We'll explore the habits, boundaries, routines and inner work that form the backbone of sustainable success.

5 **Health** Your physical and mental wellbeing is the vehicle through which you do everything else. Without it, you can't move, focus, create or thrive. Manifested action in this space is about fuelling your body, protecting your mind and building strength – not for aesthetics but for *capacity*. For stamina. For peace.

We'll talk about what it really looks like to care for your health in a way that supports – not competes with – your goals.

THE FIVE PRINCIPLES OF MANIFESTED ACTION

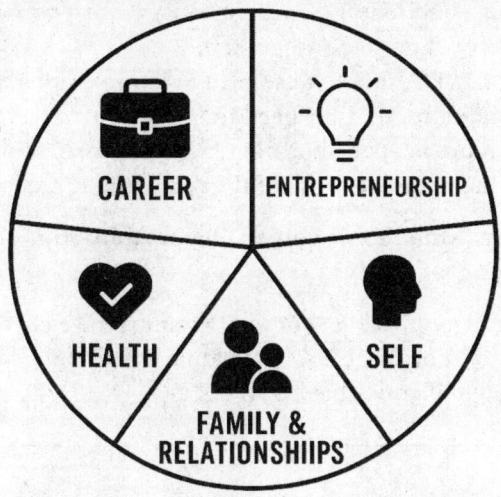

Each of these principles is connected. Your career might fund your home, but your health determines how well you show up to both. Your family life might ground you, but your business ambitions might stretch you. This book is not about compartmentalising success; it's about aligning your vision across every area of life.

So, as we continue, we'll be using the Five Principles as a lens through which you can view your own goals and take tangible, meaningful action towards them.

Manifested action is about wholeness. It's about building the life you love *in every area*, not just one. Because you don't just want a successful business. You want to enjoy it in good health, surrounded by people who get it, living in a space that reflects the version of you that you're becoming.

You want it all. And guess what?

You're allowed to have it.

Now let's get to work.

Reflection exercise: The first steps

Manifested action begins with clarity, but it's fuelled by intention. Before we move on to the next chapter, take a moment – just for you – and reflect on where you are, what you want, and what you're willing to do to get there.

You don't need a five-year plan (yet). You don't need the perfect conditions. You just need to begin.

Grab a journal, open your notes app or speak this aloud. But take the time to answer – honestly, and without judgement.

1 **What is one goal you've been thinking about or dreaming of lately?**

Be as specific as possible. Not just 'I want to be rich' or 'I want to be happy', but what does that look like in your life? What would change if you achieved it?

_____

_____

_____

2 **What does that goal look like when it's fully embedded in your reality?**

Close your eyes. Imagine waking up to that version of your life. Where are you? Who's with you? How do you feel? What's different?

_____

_____

_____

3 What actions would someone with that reality be taking daily, weekly, monthly?

Now ask yourself: are you doing those things right now? If not, what small step could you take this week to close that gap?

_____

_____

_____

4 What resources, skills or support do you need to start moving towards that goal?

This could be a course, a mentor, a financial review, or even just time. Write it down. And then ask yourself: where can I start?

_____

_____

_____

5 What might get in your way and how will you prepare for it?

Be honest here. Fear? Procrastination? Self-doubt? Family obligations? Identify the potential hurdles so they don't surprise you – and so you can plan around them.

_____

_____

_____

Your first manifested action

Before you turn the page, write down one small but intentional action you will take this week towards your goal. Just one.

It could be a phone call.
It could be booking a class.
It could be creating a budget.
It could be telling someone you trust what you're working towards.

It doesn't have to be big. It just has to be *yours*. And you have to do it.

Because this is where the dreaming ends and the building begins.

The intentional action I will take this week is:

_____

_____

_____

Setting the stage for success

Manifested action is the bridge between dreaming and doing. It reminds us that, while manifestation gives us the vision, action makes it real. By combining the two, you create a powerful force for change in your life. This book will guide you step by step, offering practical strategies, tools and inspiration to help you embrace manifested action and create the life you love. Remember, your dreams are valid, but it's your actions that will make them inevitable.

CHAPTER TWO
The Power of Positive Thinking and Visualisation

The mental blueprint of success

As a global business strategist and mentor, I (Byron) have had the privilege of working closely with more than a thousand people – entrepreneurs, professionals and changemakers alike. Between our books, mentoring programmes and online courses, Bianca and I have supported tens of thousands of individuals in pursuit of their goals. And, over the years, a pattern has emerged so clearly that it's become impossible to ignore.

It's not just about the quality of the idea.

I've seen people with phenomenal business ideas – truly game-changing concepts, backed by experience, talent and opportunity – talk themselves out of success. They second-guess every decision, spiral into self-doubt and constantly seek external validation. Their minds become battlegrounds, and before they've even launched, they're already preparing for failure.

Then you meet someone else. They've got a good idea – sometimes a fairly average one, if we're being honest. But here's the difference: they believe in it *like their life depends on it*. They show up with certainty. They're not waiting to feel confident; they move as if success is inevitable. And because of that belief, they do what most people won't: they knock on every door unashamedly. They pitch themselves at every opportunity. They build relationships, take chances, ask for help, attend the right rooms, follow up, show up and keep showing up.

And nine times out of ten? They're the ones who win.

We've seen this play out time and time again. The person with the 'okay' idea and the bulletproof mindset will often outperform the genius with doubt clouding every decision.

Bianca sees this on the corporate side, too. In her work with senior leaders, high-potential talent, and those navigating the ever-complex landscape of career progression, one thing becomes clear very quickly: it's not just about who is the most qualified. It's about who *believes* they deserve the promotion. Who believes they can operate at the next level. Who sees themselves in the role before they even get the title. Who speaks up in the meetings. Who asks for more. Who sets their intention and follows through with action.

Confidence doesn't guarantee success, but lack of belief almost always guarantees stagnation.

So let me ask you this: can you truly say the same for yourself? Do you believe in your ability to grow? To lead? To build the life you say you want?

Because if you don't – even just quietly, beneath the surface – that doubt will eventually find its way into your decisions, your habits and your results.

That's why this chapter is so important. It's not about pretending everything is perfect, or blindly 'thinking positive' like it's a spiritual life hack. It's about rewiring your internal dialogue. The mind is a powerful tool, capable of shaping our reality in profound ways. Our thoughts and beliefs influence not only how we perceive the world but also the actions we take and the outcomes we achieve. Positive thinking and visualisation are two practices that harness the potential of the mind. It's about visualising the reality you want so clearly that your mind can no longer accept anything less. It's about building the mental blueprint of success – because if it doesn't exist in your mind, it's highly unlikely it'll exist in your life. We want to delve into the science behind these practices, exploring how they can empower us to achieve our goals and live our dreams.

The science of positivity

Positive thinking is more than just being cheerful or wearing rose-tinted glasses; it's a deliberate, daily discipline. It's the conscious decision to look for solutions when problems feel overwhelming. It's choosing hope over fear, intention over reaction. And, scientifically, it has far more impact than most people realise.

Neuroscience tells us that our brains are *malleable*. Through a process called neuroplasticity, the brain is constantly reshaping itself based on our thoughts, habits and behaviours. When we repeatedly engage in positive thinking, we begin to strengthen neural pathways associated with clarity, confidence, resilience and creative problem-solving.

Dr Barbara Fredrickson, a leading psychologist in this space, developed the 'Broaden-and-Build' theory, which suggests that positive emotions literally expand our capacity to think clearly and build psychological resources. Joy, gratitude, hope – these aren't just feel-good emotions. They *broaden* our attention span, make us more open to new ideas, help us connect more deeply with others, and allow us to *build* the kind of mental and emotional reserves we need to thrive in life and business.

Bianca and I have seen this play out in our own lives countless times. From the early stages of our romantic relationship, what drew us to each other wasn't just shared interests or ambition, it was a shared mindset. We both carried the belief that bigger, better and bolder was always possible. That mindset became the foundation for not just our relationship but for every business we've built since.

We've faced challenges – financial, emotional, operational, you name it. But we chose, again and again, to view those moments not as dead ends but as detours. We didn't always get it right, but we always *believed* there was a way through. That belief shaped our behaviour. It got us into the right rooms with the right people; it got us saying yes to the right opportunities, and showing up even when things felt uncertain.

And the science backs this up.

Positive thinking doesn't mean ignoring problems – it means seeing beyond them. It rewires the brain to look for opportunities rather than dangers. You've felt this before, even if you didn't know it: that moment when a single phone call, a favourite meal, a piece of music or a sudden happy memory completely shifts your emotional state. It's your brain responding to stimuli that spark dopamine and serotonin – neurotransmitters that promote motivation, calm, focus and creativity.

But just as we can wire our minds towards opportunity, we can just as easily wire them towards defeat. Negative thoughts, when left unchallenged, can become habitual. They narrow your perspective, restrict your thinking, and make it harder to take bold action. Doubt, fear, imposter syndrome – they're like viruses in the system, shrinking your capacity to see beyond your current situation. They create *mental cages*, and before long, you stop even looking for the exit.

That's why shifting to a positive mindset is so critical – not just for your mental health, but for your outcomes. It's not about pretending bad things don't happen. It's about refusing to give those things the final word.

Your mindset is the software your action runs on. If the system is corrupted with negativity, the output will always be limited.

So, yes, you need to take action. But, before that, you need to *believe* that action will count. That it's worth it. That you're worth it.

That's where positive thinking becomes the first true step in manifested action.

The power of visualisation: What visualisation really means

Let's be honest, visualisation often gets a bad rap. It's been reduced to wishful thinking in some circles. Picture this: someone sitting on the edge of their bed, eyes closed, imagining a better life, hoping it'll somehow drop through the ceiling. And yes, there's *some* value in that. But let me be very clear.

Visualisation isn't magic. It's mental preparation.

It's about creating a clear picture of your goal – not just so it looks good in your mind, but so your mind starts believing it's *possible*. And when your brain starts believing it's possible, you start acting like it is. You speak differently. You move differently. You make decisions from a place of alignment, not fear.

This isn't fluff. This is rooted in real neuroscience. Athletes have used mental rehearsal for decades. Muhammad Ali said, 'I am the greatest,' long before the world believed it, because *he saw it*. Olympic swimmer Michael Phelps mentally rehearsed every stroke of his races – including what he would do if his goggles filled with water (which actually happened in the 2008 Beijing Olympics, and he still won gold). Formula One drivers, elite performers, CEOs – visualisation is their mental gym.

They train for their outcomes before they ever set foot on the track, the stage or the boardroom floor.

When you can see the future you want with such clarity that your mind starts to blur the line between imagination and reality, that's when visualisation starts to work its power. But, again, this only works if you're willing to back that vision with *action*.

And I'll be honest with you, Bianca and I didn't always have this level of clarity when it came to visualisation. When we wrote our first book, *Self Made*, we were just thrilled to be published. Truly. We'd landed a deal with one of the biggest publishing houses in the world, and our main focus at the time was building our personal brand, getting copies into the hands of people who needed them, and hopefully earning out our advance.

We weren't thinking about bestseller lists. We hadn't visualised billboards. We were still operating from the perspective of, 'Wow, we've made it into print!'

But once *Self Made* started building momentum, something shifted. We began to see more clearly. To think bigger. We asked ourselves, *What's next?* And that's when we visualised a new goal – one that felt audacious at the time.

We said, 'Our next book will be a *Sunday Times* bestseller. And it will be on a billboard.'

That wasn't just a dream – it became a directive.

We didn't sit back and wait. We poured ourselves into writing *The Business Survival Kit*. We made sure it was not only valuable, but also relevant, practical and needed. And when it came time to launch, we didn't just send out a few emails and hope for the best. We created strategy. We activated our community. We asked people not just to buy for themselves but to gift copies to friends, clients, schools and charities. We rallied the troops with intention.

And then one day, the call came.

The Business Survival Kit had made the *Sunday Times* Bestseller List – not just once, but in both the Non-Fiction and Business categories. And there we were, standing in Charing Cross Station, looking up at a massive digital billboard with our names and our work in lights.

Now, you can call that luck if you want. You can call it marketing. You can even call it good timing.

But we call it manifested action.

We saw it. We believed it. We worked for it. And when the moment came, it didn't feel random. It felt right. Because we had already been there – in our minds, in our plans, in our actions – long before we ever saw it in real life.

Where positivity meets realism

Let's set the record straight: positive thinking is not about delusion.

It's not about pretending everything's fine when it's falling apart. It's not about ignoring hard facts, bypassing pain, or believing that if you chant 'abundance' enough times in the mirror, your bank account will magically reflect it. That's not manifestation. That's denial with a diffuser on.

True positivity is rooted in realism. It's making the choice to stay focused on solutions when problems arise. It's having the discipline to keep your perspective intact when you're in the middle of a storm. And it's being honest enough to say, 'This is hard – but I still believe something good can come from it.'

You have to hold space for both – hope and strategy. Vision and reality. Otherwise, you risk floating so high on 'good vibes only' that you forget to look where you're stepping.

And when it comes to visualisation, that realism matters even more. You've got to visualise what *you* truly want – not what society tells you success should look like.

Let's be honest – there's a lot of noise out there. You scroll through social media and see people ticking off all the classic success boxes: G-Wagons, Birkins, business-class holidays to Bali, perfectly captioned posts about 'building their empire'. And it's easy to start thinking: *Is that what I'm supposed to want?*

I joke that Bianca has both a Birkin and a G-Wagon, and if you've ever met her, you'll know she rocks both unapologetically. But here's the difference: she wanted those things for herself, not because someone online told her she needed them to feel accomplished, but because they aligned with *her* vision of success at that stage in life. And she made it happen – through action, discipline and intention.

But that might not be your dream. And guess what? That's more than okay. Maybe success to you means building a quiet life in the countryside. Or travelling the world and working remotely. Or retiring your parents. Or starting a community project. Maybe it means getting your evenings back, having time for your kids, healing from burnout, or creating a home filled with love and laughter.

You've got to cut through the noise and ask yourself, as Bianca cheekily quotes from the Spice Girls: 'Tell me what you want, what you really really want.'[1]

That clarity is powerful. Because, once you know what *you* actually want, everything else – your mindset, your decisions, your strategy – can align around it.

And remember, even the most successful people had to start with that clarity. Oprah visualised her life long before anyone gave her a stage. She often speaks about seeing herself as being 'called to something more' and choosing to live as if it were already happening. That's not blind optimism – that's anchored faith and focused intention. Elon Musk visualised Tesla and SpaceX at a time when both seemed laughably unrealistic. He mapped out the future in his mind and moved towards it like it was inevitable.

They both knew what they wanted. They saw it. Then they built it.

Visualising your future isn't about fantasising; it's about focusing. And focusing only works when you're being honest with yourself about what you're really working towards.

So before you print out pictures for your vision board, pause and ask yourself: *is this what I want or what I think I should want?*

Strip it back. Get still. Shut out the noise. What kind of life do you want to wake up to? What kind of work feels good in your soul? What does success *feel* like, not just *look* like?

Because the more honest you are in your visualisation, the more powerful your action will become.

Techniques for harnessing positive thinking and visualisation

Positive thinking and visualisation aren't just concepts, they're practices. They're skills you can develop and refine over time. And, like any meaningful habit, they require repetition, intention and the willingness to try, even when it feels unfamiliar.

If you want to integrate positivity and visualisation into your life – not just as a once-a-year vision-board ritual, but as part of how you operate day to day – here are five techniques to get you started.

1. REFRAME NEGATIVE THOUGHTS

Negative self-talk can quietly sabotage even the most talented person. It creeps in subtly: 'I'm not ready,' 'I'm not good enough,' or 'I always mess things up.' The problem isn't just the thought – it's what you do with it.

Reframing is about challenging that voice and asking, 'Is this really true?' More often than not, it isn't. Instead of saying, 'I'm terrible at public speaking,' try, 'I'm improving my speaking skills every time I practise.'

In our early days as entrepreneurs, we had to learn this skill quickly. There were moments – pitches, launches, transitions into new sectors – when fear crept in. But we learned to focus on what we *could* do, not what might go wrong. That shift in perspective became our silent engine, keeping us moving even when confidence was low.

2. PRACTISE GRATITUDE

Gratitude isn't a fluffy, feel-good exercise – it's a focus tool. When you train your mind to recognise what's good, it becomes easier to believe that more good is possible.

Start or end your day by listing three things you're grateful for. They don't have to be groundbreaking – a productive meeting, a good cup of coffee, or a moment of peace all count. This practice rewires your brain to default towards appreciation, not lack.

We've found that gratitude has strengthened our mindsets and our relationship. Whether it's acknowledging small business wins or simply appreciating each other's consistency, gratitude reminds us why we started and grounds us in what matters most.

3. CREATE A VISION BOARD

A vision board is a visual reminder of your goals, aspirations and the life you're building. It's not just arts and crafts – it's visual clarity in a distracted world.

Find images, quotes, symbols or even physical items that represent your vision. Then put it somewhere you'll see it daily. But don't just look – *feel*. Connect with the emotion behind each image. Imagine how it feels to *live* that life.

Before we got married, we created our first joint vision board. It was a mix of personal goals – travel, a future home, a thriving relationship – and professional goals, like writing books and speaking on global stages. Today, many of those visions have come to life. That board served as a visual contract between the future we wanted and the action we were willing to take.

4. USE GUIDED VISUALISATION EXERCISES

Spend 5–10 minutes a day imagining your future as if it's already here. Close your eyes. Engage every sense.

Want a promotion? Picture the email arriving in your inbox. Imagine the handshake in the meeting room. Hear your new title being announced. Feel the excitement in your chest as you call someone you love to tell them. This isn't fantasy – it's mental rehearsal. And the brain doesn't differentiate much between a vividly imagined scenario and a real one. You're teaching your nervous system to become comfortable with success.

The more you do this, the more natural it becomes, and the more prepared you'll be when opportunity knocks.

5. ANCHOR POSITIVE EMOTIONS

Create rituals that evoke a positive emotional state. That could mean playing a powerful song in the morning, having a mantra that grounds you, or wearing something that makes you feel focused and sharp.

These small anchors create an association in your brain. Over time, your mind connects these activities with confidence, clarity and forward motion. It might sound simple, but it's remarkably effective. Your environment and your habits are constantly shaping your mindset, so make them intentional.

You don't need to do all five of these overnight. Pick one. Practise it. Then layer in another.

Remember, this is about *priming your mind* for action. And when your mindset is working *with* you – not against you – you'll be amazed how much faster your goals come into reach.

From vision to reality: The Jim Carrey cheque effect

There's perhaps no more legendary example of visualisation in action than the story of Jim Carrey and the $10 million cheque.

Before he was a household name, before *Ace Ventura* or *The Mask*, Jim Carrey was a struggling actor – broke, unknown and trying to make his way in Los Angeles. One night, he drove up to Mulholland Drive, parked his car overlooking the city, and visualised the life he wanted. He imagined being one of the most sought-after comedic actors in the world. He saw the crowds, the success, the films. And then he wrote himself a cheque for $10 million 'for acting services rendered', postdated it for five years in the future, and kept it in his wallet.

Five years later, almost to the day, he received a cheque for $10 million for his role in *Dumb and Dumber*.

Now, did the cheque in his wallet land him the role? Of course not. But it *did* give him clarity. It anchored his vision. And that clarity fuelled the action he took every single day – the auditions, the rejections, the relentless belief that what he saw in his mind could one day be real.

Visualisation is not about living in fantasy – it's about fuelling your reality.

That's what we're inviting you to do throughout this book. Not just to dream but to design. To build a bridge between where you are and where you want to be. And to let visualisation be one of the tools that strengthens every step you take on that path.

Applying visualisation across the Five Principles

As we explained in Chapter 1, the five core areas of your life – career, entrepreneurship, family and relationships, self and health – are the foundation upon which your success is built. Let's explore how positivity and visualisation can serve you within each principle.

1 **Career** See yourself in the job you want – not just the title, but how you behave in that role. Imagine contributing to strategy, leading teams, being respected and valued. Visualise walking into that office (virtual or real) with confidence. Use that clarity to start taking steps now: learn the skill, ask for the mentorship, show up like the future version of you already exists.

2 **Entrepreneurship** Visualise your ideal customer discovering your product or service. Picture the sale, the growth, the brand expanding. But also imagine the resilience you'll need – the late nights, the hard conversations, the big risks. Positivity here isn't about avoiding difficulty; it's about staying focused through it. Keep the bigger vision alive while staying grounded in the daily execution.

3 **Family and relationships** What do you want your relationships to feel like? Visualise the love, the peace, the quality time. If you're a parent, picture the kind of connection you want with your children. If you're manifesting partnership, see the energy and safety of that bond. Let those visions guide how you show up for the people you love today.

4 **Self** This principle is often the most overlooked. Who are you becoming? What kind of person do you want to be when no one's watching? Visualise yourself confident, disciplined, joyful, resilient. See your boundaries being honoured. See your goals being achieved. Then live in alignment with that image – even when it feels uncomfortable.

5 **Health** Health is more than fitness – it's energy, mobility, mental strength, emotional balance. Visualise yourself thriving in your body: energetic, rested, strong. What routines support that version of you? What does that person

eat? How do they sleep, move, think? Start shifting your daily habits to match the version of you who already has what you want.

Visualisation becomes powerful when it's personal. When it's yours.

And once your vision becomes non-negotiable, your actions start falling into line.

Reflection exercise: Priming your mind for action

By now, you understand that positive thinking and visualisation aren't abstract luxuries – they're the groundwork for everything you want to build. But knowledge without action is just inspiration with nowhere to go.

So before you close this chapter, take a few minutes to check in with yourself and put these tools into motion.

You'll need a quiet moment, something to write with, and honesty.

1 What is one negative belief you've been repeating – out loud or silently – that no longer serves you?

Write it down. Then reframe it into a new, empowering thought. Repeat it daily until it becomes second nature.

_____

_____

_____

2 What is a goal you're working towards in one of the Five Principles?

Be specific. What does success look like in that area? Now close your eyes and visualise it – clearly. See it. Feel it. Anchor it in your imagination.

_____

_____

_____

3 What's one small action you can take this week to move that vision closer to reality?

Book the meeting. Start the course. Make the call. Commit to it. It doesn't need to be huge, it just needs to move you forward.

_____

_____

_____

4 What daily practice will you implement to support your mindset?

Will you journal in the morning? Play an empowering song? Create a vision board? Choose one ritual that will keep your focus sharp and your energy high.

_____

_____

_____

Your manifested action prompt:

This week, I will choose my thoughts with intention.
I will act as though my success is inevitable.
I will visualise the future I desire, and take one aligned step towards it every day.

Setting the stage for success

Visualisation is not about fantasy – it's about focus.

Positive thinking and visualisation are not magic tricks; they are tools that prepare your mind and body for success. By adopting these practices, you create an environment where possibilities thrive. When combined with manifested action, they become a powerful force for achieving your goals.

It's about putting your mind where your future is, so you can bring it into the present with clarity and conviction. And positive thinking isn't about ignoring life's challenges; it's about refusing to let them define you.

For us, manifested action is a journey we continue to walk every day – in our businesses, our relationships and our personal growth. These practices have given us not only the tools we need to succeed but also the joy of celebrating the process together. The life you envision is not only possible but inevitable when backed by purposeful action.

The more you practise these principles, the more your life will begin to reflect them.

You don't have to have it all figured out. You just have to begin.

Now, let's explore how to take this foundation and build upon it in the next chapter.

CHAPTER THREE
Setting Goals and Making Plans

When the world shifts, so must the plan

Goals are the stepping stones that transform dreams into reality. Without them, even the grandest aspirations can feel elusive and overwhelming. But what happens when the world as you know it changes overnight – when everything you've built, planned for or visualised is suddenly upended? That's exactly what happened to us during the global pandemic.

I (Bianca) have been a speaker for more than 14 years. I've travelled across continents sharing stages with global brands, business leaders and thousands of brilliant minds. Speaking has always been more than a profession for me – it's a passion. A calling. And, like many professionals, I had my year mapped out with meticulous precision. In 2020, I had a six-figure pipeline of international engagements with some of the most respected organisations in the world. The calendar was full, the opportunities were flowing, and our mentoring business – delivered primarily in person – was thriving.

Then the world shut down.

In what felt like the blink of an eye, every single speaking engagement was cancelled. Our mentoring model, which had always been based on face-to-face delivery, became instantly obsolete. For a moment, it felt like the ground had shifted beneath our feet – and in many ways, it had.

But here's the thing: we had a choice. To freeze . . . or to adapt.

And we chose to adapt.

Re-evaluating goals in a time of crisis

We could have mourned what was lost – and in some ways, we did. But very quickly, we turned our attention to what could be created. We took the opportunity to reimagine not only our delivery model, but also our goals, our client base and even our lifestyle. We transitioned our mentoring services online, something we'd never fully considered before. Suddenly, we weren't bound by postcodes or train lines. We were mentoring clients across the UK, across Europe – even as far afield as the UAE and Ghana – from the comfort of our own home.

The pandemic didn't just force us to pivot – it pushed us to refine. To get even clearer on what we offered, who we served, and how we could future-proof our business and our goals.

Because here's the truth that doesn't get posted on Instagram: real goal-setting is not just about ambition. It's not about journaling pretty words or making a cute to-do list for the New Year. It's about context. Clarity, yes, but also awareness.

Who are you serving?
What do they need – now, not five years ago?
What's the economic environment doing?
Where are the opportunities and where are the risks?

If you don't answer those questions, your goals may sound impressive but they'll lack relevance. And in business, relevance is everything.

That's why I always say that lived experience matters far more than borrowed wisdom. You can scroll for hours and see stories of so-called 'overnight' success. But what you don't see is the context. The ten years of quiet hustle. The market timing. The connections. The privilege. The plan.

And that's why, when I speak around the world – whether to entrepreneurs, executives or future leaders – I share my two buzz-words for the year. For the last four years, they've been the same:

Purpose and Clarity.

If you don't have those two things defined, how can you set mean-ingful goals? And if your goals aren't meaningful, how on earth will you stay motivated when things get hard?

- **Purpose** gives your goals direction. It's the *why*. The fire in your belly.
- **Clarity** gives your goals structure. It's the *how*. The steps that keep you grounded and moving forward.

So, as we move through this chapter, I want to challenge you not just to think about what you want, but to *really* consider why you want it, who it serves, and what it requires of you.

This isn't about creating a Pinterest board of dreams. This is about building a strategic, values-led roadmap to the life you want – and preparing yourself to meet it head-on.

How to set goals that actually work

If there's one thing I want you to take from this section, it's this:

Vague goals get vague results. Clear goals create movement.

So many people say they want more – more money, more time, more growth, more impact – but they never define what 'more' actually means. They leave their future in the fog, then wonder why they can't find their way forward.

I've seen it over and over again – people who are ambitious, talented, driven . . . but stuck. Not because they don't care, or because they're not capable, but because they don't have *clarity*. And without clarity, there's no action. Without action, there's no traction.

It's why I say all the time: a goal without a plan is just a wish. And wishes won't build the life you want.

Rethinking SMART goals

You've probably come across SMART goals before. It's one of the most popular frameworks for goal-setting, and for good reason – it offers structure. But structure without soul won't carry you far.

Traditionally, SMART stands for:

Specific   **R**ealistic
Measurable   **T**ime-bound
Achievable

But let me say this loud and clear: we do not subscribe to 'realistic'. That word alone has clipped more wings than we can count.

What's realistic to your neighbour, your colleague, your parents or your partner might be entirely different from what's possible for you. Many of the most powerful inventions and boldest achievements in history started as ideas people thought were ridiculous.

The Wright brothers envisioned powered flight before there was even a vocabulary for it.

Marie Van Brittan Brown, driven by safety concerns, designed the prototype that would evolve into the home CCTV system – decades before the 'smart home' was a thing.

Tim Berners-Lee built the foundations of the modern internet with nothing but vision and belief. Now, we can't imagine life without it.

If they had stopped at 'realistic', none of us would be where we are now.

So, let's remix it. SMART still stands, but with intention, fire and vision behind every letter.

SMART (the *Manifested Action* edition)

Specific. Your goal must be clear and focused. 'I want to be successful' is vague. 'I want to launch an online coaching platform for women in tech by January' is specific.

Measurable. You must be able to track it. Quantify it. What does success *look like*? Is it £50k in revenue? Three new clients per month? A published book? Progress becomes visible when it's measurable.

Achievable. It should be something you can actively work towards from where you are now, even if you're not fully ready yet. Growth happens when the goal is within reach, but not within comfort.

Risky/Radical. This is where it gets exciting. Your goal should stretch your imagination. Challenge what you thought was possible. If it doesn't make you a bit nervous, it's probably not big enough.

Time-bound. A deadline turns 'someday' into a date. When will you do this by? Give it a timeline so you can plan backwards and hold yourself accountable.

A step-by-step guide to goal-setting
(the Manifested Action *way)*

Let's walk this through in real terms. Here's the process we use with clients and mentees and in our own planning:

1 **Start with the vision.** What do you actually want? Not what looks good on social media. Not what your peers are doing. Go quiet and ask yourself: what would truly excite me?

   Write without judgement. Let it be wild if it needs to be. You can refine later.

2 **Be ruthlessly specific.** If your goal is to 'buy a house', go deeper. How many bedrooms? Detached or semi? Where? What kind of feeling do you want when you walk through the door? The more detail you give your brain, the more focused your actions will become.

3 **Put a number on it.** Attach something tangible – cost, percentages, units, dates, deadlines. You can't move towards a fog. Measurability gives your brain a bull's-eye.

4 **Break it down.** Every bold goal has smaller steps. Let's say your big goal is to launch a new product. Your sub-goals might include:

   ● Research audience pain points.
   ● Build your prototype.
   ● Run a pilot.
   ● Finalise branding and messaging.
   ● Set up payment and delivery system.
   ● Launch.

   Once you have the steps, assign them dates. Put them in your calendar. Make them real.

5 **Identify your roadblocks.** What could throw you off course? Time? Fear? Resources? Write them down and then create counter-strategies. If you know what might go wrong, you're halfway to staying on track.
6 **Create a support system.** You do not have to do this alone. Who can hold you accountable? Encourage you? Challenge you? Who can you hire, partner with, learn from or lean on? Success is rarely a solo sport.
7 **Embody the goal.** Visualise it daily. Speak it out loud. Act like the version of you who already has it. The more your habits reflect the destination, the faster you'll get there.

In the next section, we'll show you what this looked like in real time – how our goals evolved as our lives, business and vision expanded across borders.

But before we go there, just know this:

The right goal, with the right energy and the right structure, is not just something you achieve.
It's something that transforms you in the process.

When goals grow with you

There's this myth we need to let go of: that once you set a goal, you must stick with it no matter what.

That's not discipline. That's rigidity. And rigidity will break you long before it builds you.

The truth is that life evolves – and your goals should evolve with it.

Sometimes your environment changes. Sometimes you change. And what once made perfect sense might no longer fit the season you're in. That's not failure. That's growth.

In fact, the ability to adapt your goals is a sign of maturity, not weakness. It means you're paying attention. It means you're in tune with who you are now, not who you were when you first wrote down the goal.

Let me give you a real-life example.

As I shared earlier in this chapter, before the pandemic, I was travelling the world as a speaker, working with high-profile clients, building both mine and Byron's businesses at pace. We had a beautiful home, a busy calendar and a goal to scale up what we were already doing.

Then everything changed.

Almost overnight, my six-figure pipeline of speaking work vanished. Our in-person mentoring model was no longer viable. Like millions of people around the world, we found ourselves in a global moment of pause.

But that pause became a pivot.

We adapted. We moved our services online. We reached people across the UK, Europe, Africa and beyond – from the comfort of our home. Suddenly, a new idea started to take shape: what if home didn't have to be the UK? What if we could live, raise our family and grow our businesses from anywhere in the world?

So we travelled – Ghana, the UAE, Thailand, parts of Europe. We explored. And with every trip, our goals shifted again. What started as a plan to simply ride out the pandemic became a vision for a completely different kind of life.

We worked towards a residential visa in the UAE. We planned for a dual-location lifestyle – splitting our time between the UK and the Middle East. And then, when we became parents, our priorities evolved again. We returned to the UK for community and family support during those early months of parenthood, but after a trip back to the UAE, it became clear.

This wasn't just a travel goal anymore. It was a life goal.

And we were ready to go all in.

By the time this book is published, we'll be living in the UAE full-time. But we wouldn't be here if we'd clung rigidly to our pre-2020 plans.

So let me say this clearly: your goals are allowed to change.

That change might be triggered by a crisis – like a global pandemic.
It might be prompted by a new chapter – becoming a parent, changing careers, moving house.
It might come from a simple moment of reflection – realising that what once felt exciting now feels misaligned.

None of these are reasons to feel shame. They are signs that you are *present*. That you are growing. That you are in touch with your evolving needs, values and priorities.

Adaptability is not optional. It's essential.

Because the alternative is to chase outdated goals that no longer fit. And let me tell you – few things are more exhausting than achieving a goal that no longer fulfils you.

That's why we regularly revisit our vision. We ask each other:

- Does this still excite us?
- Is this still aligned with where we're heading?
- Have we outgrown this idea or has it grown into something else?

Sometimes the goal just needs refining. Other times, it needs replacing. But in both cases, it's not about giving up; it's about levelling up.

And if you're reading this thinking, 'That's me' – maybe you've been holding on to an old goal because you think letting it go means you've failed – this is your permission to shift. To upgrade. To evolve.

Because here's the thing: you are not the same person you were last year. So why should your goals be?

Creating big goals and making them happen

Big goals, like moving to another country, come with their challenges. It required meticulous planning – from securing visas and choosing the right home to navigating education options for our child. But big goals also inspire growth. They push you out of your comfort zone and into a space where you're required to think strategically and act decisively.

We want readers to see this as a testament to the power of setting bold goals. Whether it's starting a new business, pivoting in your career, or making a significant lifestyle change, the first step is creating a vision for what you want. Then, break it down into actionable steps.

Ask yourself:

- What do I truly want, and why does it matter?
- What steps can I take today to move closer to my goal?
- What obstacles might I face, and how can I prepare for them?

These questions became our guiding framework during this transformative time.

Applying goal-setting to the Five Principles

One of the most powerful ways to stay intentional with your goals is to build them around the areas that matter most to your life. These are what Byron and I call the Five Principles – the foundations that almost every person is building their dreams upon, consciously or not.

When you set goals across these five areas, you create alignment. You stop living in silos – working on your career while neglecting your health, or building a business while ignoring your relationships. Instead, you start designing a life that's whole, grounded and rich with meaning.

Let's break them down.

1. CAREER

For professionals, career goals often get boxed in – promotion, salary increase, maybe a new title. And while those things matter, what matters more is alignment. Is your role helping you grow or just keeping you busy? Are you leading or simply surviving the workday?

Ask yourself:

- Where do I want to be in 12–24 months?
- What role or path aligns with my long-term vision?
- What skills or relationships do I need to get there?

SMART example:

S: Apply for senior project management roles within my sector.
M: Secure three interviews in the next six months.
A: Update CV, get feedback from a mentor, start networking.
R: Radical if you've been overlooked before, but that's the point.
T: Have a new role secured by Q3.

And remember: your job is not your identity. It's a vehicle. Make sure it's going somewhere you actually want to go.

2. ENTREPRENEURSHIP

Entrepreneurial goals often come with high stakes and big emotions, especially if you're starting something from scratch. It's easy to get caught up in the vision without locking down the *steps*.

We always ask our mentees:

- What's the problem you solve?
- Who's paying for the solution?
- What does success look like (not just sound like)?

SMART example:

S: Launch a coaching offer for mid-level female leaders.
M: Sign ten clients at £1,000 by year-end.
A: Build offer, test with beta group, refine messaging.
R: Risky? Yes. But the upside is scalable and life-changing.
T: Launch campaign by September, full client roster by December.

If you're not measuring the right things – profit, sustainability, impact – you're not running a business, you're running in circles.

3. FAMILY AND RELATIONSHIPS

Family and relationship goals are often the hardest to define, but they're the most important to be intentional about. Whether it's parenting, nurturing your marriage, building a chosen family or improving your home life, these goals deserve clarity, too.

Ask yourself:

- What do I want more of in my relationships?
- What kind of partner/parent/friend do I want to be?
- What do connection and quality time look like in this season?

SMART example:

S: Build stronger communication with my teenage son.
M: Enjoy weekly one-on-one activities or chats without devices.
A: Schedule time, set tone, explore shared interests.

R: Radical? For some families, yes, but deeply worthwhile.
T: Start next week, continue for three months, then review.

Your home is your foundation. Build it with care.

4. SELF

This is where most people forget to set goals and then wonder why they feel disconnected. Self-development isn't selfish. It's strategy. Who you're becoming matters more than what you're producing.
Ask yourself:

- What kind of life do I want to wake up to?
- What am I currently tolerating that doesn't serve me?
- What makes me feel most like myself?

SMART example:

S: Build a peaceful morning routine that supports my mindset.
M: Meditate and journal for 15 minutes each weekday.
A: Choose tools/apps, protect time, be consistent.
R: Radical for those constantly 'on', but transformative.
T: Implement within the next seven days.

If you want to create a life you love, you need to become someone who honours your own energy, time and values.

5. HEALTH

Physical and mental wellbeing aren't extras – they are essential. Without health, you can't lead, grow or serve well. And your goals around wellbeing need to be just as structured as your career plans.
Ask yourself:

- What would thriving feel like in my body and mind?
- What habits support that vision?
- What have I been avoiding that needs attention?

SMART example:

S: Improve physical strength and reduce stress.
M: Take three strength-training sessions and two walks weekly.

A: Join gym or online programme, block out time.
R: Radical for a hectic schedule, but your body is the foundation.
T: Start Monday, track progress for 12 weeks.

Wellness isn't a trend. It's a non-negotiable.

These Five Principles are not a to-do list – they're a *lens*. Use them to build goals that reflect your whole life, not just one side of it.

Because balance isn't about doing everything at once. It's about knowing what matters *right now* and honouring it with clarity and action.

Reflection exercise: Set the vision, plan the path – your *Manifested Action* goal map

By now, you've seen that goal-setting isn't just about writing something down and crossing your fingers. It's about designing a life with clarity, purpose and momentum.

But before you rush to fill in boxes or build a new timeline, pause.

This is your moment to check in – *not* with what you think you should want, but with what's actually calling you forward.

Grab your notebook, journal or goal planner and take a quiet moment to complete these prompts. Reflect honestly – this is for you.

1 What is **one bold, exciting, even slightly scary goal** you want to achieve this year? Be as specific as possible. This is your 'R' – *risky*, radical, but *real* to you.

_____

_____

_____

2 **Why do you want this?** Go beyond surface motivation. What will this goal change in your life? What does it mean for your legacy, your peace, your growth?

_____

_____

3 **Apply the SMART framework** (your version):
Specific:

_____

Measurable:

_____

Achievable:

_____

Risky/Radical:

_____

Time-bound:

_____

4 **Break it into three key milestones.** What are the big markers on the path to your goal?

• _____

• _____

• _____

5 **What's the first step you can take this week?** It doesn't have to be massive. Just real. Action builds confidence.

_____

_____

_____

6 **What might get in the way?** Be honest: mindset, time, fear, resources. Now, write one thing you'll do to navigate each.

_____

_____

_____

7 **Who can support you on this journey?** A mentor? Partner? Accountability buddy? Don't go it alone – identify your people.

_____

_____

_____

Setting the stage for success

The goals you set today are not just tasks to tick off – they are declarations. They're blueprints for the life you're building, and evidence of the belief you're willing to back with action.

And remember, your goals aren't meant to trap you in an old version of yourself. They're meant to grow with you. Evolve with you. Challenge you. Stretch you.

Celebrate you.

You don't have to have it all figured out. You just have to begin – with intention, courage, and one action at a time.

'If the plan doesn't work, change the plan – never the goal.'

Unknown (but wise)

CHAPTER FOUR
Overcoming Fear and Doubt

Fear is not the enemy

Fear and doubt are two of the most insidious roadblocks on the path to achieving our goals. As we sit in the midst of planning our move to the UAE full-time, these emotions are ever-present, whispering questions about the unknown and the unpredictable future. Even with all the planning and preparation, we know stepping into the next chapter of our lives will require courage, resilience and trust in our vision.

And that's the paradox of fear: it shows up strongest right when we're on the edge of something important. Right when we're preparing to step into more.

So let's begin this chapter by being honest: fear is not always the enemy.

At its core, fear is a survival mechanism. From an evolutionary standpoint, fear is what kept us alive. It's what told our ancestors to run from danger, avoid poisonous food or seek shelter in a storm. It originates in the amygdala, the part of the brain that processes emotions and assesses threats. When it senses danger – real or perceived – it activates the body's 'fight or flight' response. Your heart races, your palms sweat, your breathing quickens and you become hyper-alert.

But in the modern world, danger doesn't always come with flashing lights. Sometimes, danger wears a suit and shows up as the fear of rejection. Sometimes it's the worry of financial instability. Sometimes it's the doubt that creeps in when you're about to speak up in a meeting, pitch your business idea, or move your family across the world.

What's changed is that the fear we face today is rarely life-threatening, even though it can still feel that way – because our brain doesn't always distinguish between *real danger* and *perceived threat*. And that's where the challenge lies.

From a psychological perspective, fear can be instilled early. Childhood experiences, family conditioning, cultural expectations – all these shape how we see risk, how we interpret failure and how we respond to uncertainty. If you were praised only when you played it safe, or punished when you made mistakes, you may have learned to associate ambition with danger. Doubt becomes your defence mechanism. Fear becomes the strategy that stops you from being disappointed – or so it seems.

But here's the problem: fear might protect you from pain, but it also blocks you from possibility.

It narrows your vision. It shrinks your confidence. It talks you out of your calling before you've even taken the first step.

And yet, when we understand fear, when we get curious about it rather than being controlled by it, it can become a powerful tool. Fear can be a signal that you're expanding. That you're reaching into a new space. That you care deeply about what you're doing. In those moments, fear doesn't mean stop. It means *prepare*.

Because courage is not the absence of fear. It's the decision to move forward, despite it.

Right now, we are navigating one of the most significant transitions of our lives. Moving our family from the UK to the UAE is not something we're doing lightly. It's taken years of vision, strategy and real work. But that doesn't mean it's without fear. We've had questions. *What if we've made the wrong decision? What if we don't feel at home? What if things don't go as planned?*

But for every *what if* rooted in fear, we're asking another: *what if this is the best decision we've ever made?*

This chapter is for the part of you that's scared to take that next step. It's for the voice inside that's unsure, unsettled or quietly panicking behind the scenes. It's here to remind you that fear doesn't have to be the driver; it can sit in the back while you take the wheel.

Let's begin by exploring what fear and doubt really sound like, how they disguise themselves, and what you can do to take your power back.

Embracing the fear of the unknown

There's a particular kind of fear that shows up just before a big leap. It's not the scream-in-the-face kind of panic; it's quieter than that. More internal. It whispers rather than shouts. It's the fear of stepping into something new without knowing how it's going to unfold. It's the fear of not having all the answers.

We're living in that space right now.

As we finalise plans for our move to the UAE, we're excited but also aware of everything that lies outside our control. For everything from cultural differences and logistical challenges to schooling, business registration, healthcare and, of course, the emotional adjustment of creating a new home – there's no blueprint. And that can be unnerving.

But we're choosing to embrace it. Not because we're fearless, but because we've come to understand something important.

Growth and fear often arrive hand in hand. The presence of fear is a clue that you're entering new territory – and that's where the magic tends to happen.

And we're not alone in that experience.

A British leap: Clara Amfo's honest fear

When BBC Radio 1 presenter and broadcaster Clara Amfo took a very public step outside of her usual professional role – sharing her emotional and deeply personal speech in the aftermath of George Floyd's murder – she admitted that fear nearly stopped her. She didn't know how her speech would be received, whether she would be praised, criticised, silenced or ignored. But she spoke anyway. She used her platform with vulnerability and clarity, and her words resonated around the world.

That moment wasn't planned. It wasn't comfortable. But it was powerful.

Later, Clara shared that embracing the unknown and using her voice changed not only how the world saw her but also how she saw herself. Her fear didn't disappear – it transformed into purpose.

A stateside risk: Dwayne 'The Rock' Johnson's reinvention

You might know Dwayne Johnson as a global action hero and entrepreneur, but before Hollywood, before millions of followers, before his tequila brand and motivational Instagram captions, he was a professional wrestler facing a career-ending identity shift.

When he left wrestling to pursue acting, he was told repeatedly that he wouldn't make it. Too big. Too niche. Too typecast. Agents and producers dismissed him. Even fans weren't sure what to make of it.

But he believed in his vision and took the leap anyway.

In interviews, Dwayne has spoken openly about the fear of starting again, the financial insecurity that followed, and the emotional weight of uncertainty. But he committed to his new path and embraced the learning curve. And as we know, the leap paid off.

Fear didn't leave him. He just moved anyway.

Our story, in real time

We're in that same space now – holding both excitement and uncertainty in each hand. Finalising documents, thinking about childcare, researching healthcare systems, analysing the cost of living, running businesses remotely while parenting – it's all new. And, of course, the questions show up:

- What if it's the wrong move?
- What if we miss our support system?
- What if we don't feel at home?
- What if things go wrong?

But for every fear, we offer ourselves a counter-thought:

- What if this is exactly what our family needs?
- What if we grow faster and deeper than ever before?
- What if we find a community that feels expansive and aligned?

Fear of the unknown is natural. But staying stuck because of it is a choice.

So, instead, we lean into the unknown. We ask better questions. We seek clarity. We do the research. We make contingency plans. And then – we act.

Because clarity doesn't come before the decision. Often, clarity is the result of commitment. You don't always get to feel certain before you leap. Sometimes you leap, and certainty meets you in mid-air.

Reframing doubt

If fear is the voice that says, 'What if this goes wrong?', then doubt is the voice that whispers, 'Who do you think you are?'

Doubt creeps in quietly. It doesn't always announce itself. Sometimes it arrives in the form of hesitation. A pause. A watered-down version of your own ambition. You don't say *no*, but you do say *not yet*, *maybe later* or *let me wait until it's perfect*.

And that hesitation, when repeated over time, becomes a habit. A strategy. A safe place to hide from risk and responsibility.

But here's the thing: doubt isn't always born inside you. Often, it's passed to you, spoken over you, modelled around you.

The doubt we inherit

From the moment we start engaging with the world, we are absorbing signals. Children raised in environments where risk is feared and perfection is rewarded often learn to silence their instincts and question their desires. Even as adults, we carry these early experiences like invisible scripts.

You might hear echoes of this in your own life:

- a parent who questioned your choices out of love, but left you second-guessing everything
- a boss who dismissed your ideas in meetings, so now you hold back
- a partner who said, 'Are you sure?' one too many times
- friends who laugh off your ambition as a 'phase'

- associates who asked how that 'little business' was going
- colleagues who project their fear on to your boldness

We're not just navigating our own doubts – we're often battling the doubts that have been projected on to us.

And that's why your environment matters more than most people realise.

The influence of your circle

Take a look around you. Who are the people in your circle?

Do they fan your flames – or throw water on your ideas?
Do they challenge you to rise – or give you reasons to stay small?
Do they celebrate your growth – or subtly compete with it?

Because here's the hard truth: you can have all the vision and strategy in the world, but if your circle doesn't believe in you – or, worse, doesn't want you to succeed – you'll find yourself doubting what you once felt sure about.

This isn't just motivational talk. It's psychology.

The concept of social proof – a phenomenon well documented in behavioural science – tells us that human beings naturally seek confirmation from those around them before making decisions. It's why people read reviews before buying a product, or feel safer taking action when others are doing the same.

But social proof isn't just about products. It shows up in our dreams.

When people around you say, 'Yes, go for it,' or, 'You're more than capable,' you begin to internalise that as truth.

But when they respond with silence, sarcasm or subtle discouragement? You start questioning yourself, even if you were rock solid before.

And that's why one of the fastest ways to reduce doubt is to audit your environment.

Ask yourself:

- Who in my life makes me feel more confident, more powerful, more possible?
- Who consistently makes me shrink, explain or justify myself?
- Who is actually living in the kind of energy I want to embody?

You don't need a circle of cheerleaders who blindly agree with you, but you do need people who hold space for your growth. Who challenge you *upward*, not back into your comfort zone.

How we reframe doubt

In our own journey, doubt has shown up more times than we can count – new chapters, new countries, new business ventures, parenthood, new clients, high-risk decisions. But we've learned to shift it. To take the doubt and turn it into data. To ask better questions:

- Is this doubt based on fact or fear?
- Am I doubting myself, or am I echoing someone else's fear projected on to me?
- What's the version of this thought that would empower me instead?

Instead of 'What if I fail?' we ask, 'What if I fly?'

Instead of 'What if I'm not ready?' we ask, 'What would it take for me to feel ready?'

We reframe. We visualise. And we remind ourselves of everything we've done before that once felt impossible too.

Tools to shift doubt into direction

Here are some practical tools we use – personally and with clients – to turn doubt into drive:

1 **Identify the source.** Write down the doubt. Trace it. Where did it come from? Who said it first? Is it yours or is it inherited?

2 **Reframe the belief.** Turn 'I don't know enough' into 'I'm committed to learning what I need.' Turn 'This has never been done before' into 'I'm breaking new ground.'

3 **Give gratitude for what you've overcome.** Reflect on five times you doubted yourself and did it anyway. Let your own history be your proof.

4 **Upgrade your circle.** Limit time with people who deplete you. Prioritise those who expand you. Join networks, communities or masterminds aligned with your growth.

5 **Practise visualisation.** Close your eyes and imagine the moment you've achieved the goal you're currently doubting. Sit in that energy. Repeat daily.

Doubt will visit. That's a given. But it doesn't get to run the show. You do.

And it starts with choosing to believe in your own possibility – even when the room goes quiet.

Fear in the Five Principles

Fear doesn't look the same for everyone. And it rarely shows up in isolation. It weaves itself into different areas of our lives, wearing different masks – doubt in your abilities, fear of judgement, fear of failure, even fear of success.

That's why we want to take a moment to revisit the Five Principles – career, entrepreneurship, family and relationships, self and health – and examine how fear can manifest in each. Because once you name it, you can start to reframe it.

Let's explore each one and ask the questions that will move you forward.

1. CAREER

In the career space, fear often comes disguised as:

- staying too long in a role you've outgrown
- not applying for that promotion because you don't tick every box

- silencing your ideas in meetings because you're afraid of being wrong
- believing you've peaked before you've even truly started

Ask yourself:

- What career move have I been putting off because I fear rejection or failure?
- If I trusted my skillset completely, what would I do differently tomorrow?
- What's the worst that could happen if I asked for more?
- Who in my field inspires me, and what leap did they take that I haven't yet?

2. ENTREPRENEURSHIP

Fear in business can be paralysing. It shows up as:

- perfectionism before launching
- constant comparison with competitors
- delaying big decisions
- undercharging because you fear pricing yourself out

Ask yourself:

- What business idea have I kept on hold because I'm afraid of it failing?
- If I couldn't lose, what bold move would I make this quarter?
- Who am I not reaching out to because I fear a 'no'?
- What would my business look like if I stopped hiding?

3. FAMILY AND RELATIONSHIPS

Fear in family and relationships is often quiet but heavy:

- avoiding hard conversations
- worrying about not being a good enough parent or partner
- holding back your dreams to keep the peace
- believing you can't have success *and* a thriving home life

Ask yourself:

- Where am I playing small in my family life out of fear of rocking the boat?
- What do I fear would happen if I prioritised myself for a season?
- What conversations am I avoiding and what would change if I had them?
- Am I building the kind of family energy I want my children to inherit?

4. SELF

This is the most personal principle and often the one where fear speaks loudest:

- fear of not being enough
- fear of outgrowing your identity
- fear of being seen fully
- fear of your own potential

Ask yourself:

- What belief about myself am I holding on to that is no longer serving me?
- Where do I self-sabotage out of fear of change?
- What version of myself am I afraid to step into, and why?
- Who could I become if I stopped doubting my worth?

5. HEALTH

Fear in health often shows up as neglect:

- postponing the check-up
- avoiding movement or nutrition changes
- suppressing stress or mental health struggles
- believing 'I don't have time to be well'

Ask yourself:

- What's one health habit I'm afraid to commit to, and what's underneath that fear?

- How is fear holding me back from getting help or support?
- What does vibrant health look like for me, and what would it take to get there?
- What do I believe about my body or mind that needs to be reprogrammed?

We all carry fears in these areas, but the difference between those who move forward and those who stay stuck lies not in *whether* the fear exists but in *how* they respond to it.

And the more honest you are about where fear is living in your life, the more power you have to move through it.

Analyse risk to overcome fear and doubt

We often talk about fear like it's mysterious and uncontrollable – something that just *happens* to us. But, in many cases, fear is simply the result of unclear risk.

When you can't see what's on the other side of a decision, your brain fills the gap with worst-case scenarios. That's natural – it's the mind trying to protect you. But if left unchecked, it can stop you from making the moves that matter most.

The solution? Make the risk visible. Break it down. Assess it properly.

Because when fear is grounded in facts – not assumptions – you can respond, not just react.

The 360-degree risk review

We teach this method to clients all the time. It's not about pretending risk doesn't exist. It's about understanding which risks are worth taking and which ones can be managed better.

Here's how it works.

STEP 1: DEFINE THE DESIRE

Start by clearly stating the desire you're feeling:

- 'I want to move abroad.'

- 'I want to quit my job and go freelance.'
- 'I want to invest in a new property.'

Be honest and specific.

STEP 2: WHAT'S THE WORST THAT COULD HAPPEN?

Let's get this part out of the way early.
Ask yourself:

- If this went completely wrong, what would happen?
- How likely is that scenario, really?
- Could I recover from it, and how?

This is not about fearmongering. It's about removing the drama from the unknown. Most of the time, when you articulate the 'worst case', it becomes less terrifying.

STEP 3: WHAT'S THE BEST THAT COULD HAPPEN?

Now flip it:

- What doors could this decision open?
- What would success look and feel like?
- Who else would benefit from this move?

This step matters because fear tends to magnify failure and minimise reward. You need to intentionally expand your vision of what *could go right*.

STEP 4: WHAT'S THE COST OF DOING NOTHING?

This is the question most people ignore.

- What do I risk by staying where I am?
- What opportunities might I miss if I delay?
- How will I feel a year from now if I never try?

Sometimes, the greatest risk is not the leap – it's the stagnation.

STEP 5: MITIGATE WHAT YOU CAN

Not all risk is avoidable. But much of it is manageable.

- What can I research?
- Who can I speak to who's done it before?
- What systems, buffers or back-up plans can I put in place?

Fear loves a vague plan. But clarity is the antidote.

STEP 6: CHOOSE YOUR RISK PROFILE

Here's the truth: there is no such thing as a zero-risk life. Whether you're launching a business, moving country, changing careers or starting a family, there will always be unknowns.

The real question is:

- What level of risk am I willing to live with in exchange for the life I want?

Some risks are reckless. Others are radical but necessary. Your job is to know the difference – and move accordingly.

Our own risk review

When we decided to pursue a full-time move to the UAE, we didn't take it lightly. We reviewed every angle:

- Could we sustain our businesses remotely?
- What were the education and healthcare systems like?
- How would this change impact our one-year-old son – not just now, but in the years to come?
- What would we lose and what could we gain?

We did the work. We asked the questions. And, ultimately, we saw that the risk of *not* going – the regret of playing small – was far greater than the discomfort of transition.

So we plan to move. Not blindly. But boldly.

Risk is part of growth. But unmanaged fear doesn't have to be.

When you analyse risk properly, you reclaim your power. You stop being paralysed by the unknown, and you start stepping into your next level with intention.

Imposter syndrome and the fear of inadequacy

Sometimes fear isn't loud. It doesn't shake the ground or scream in your face. Sometimes it's subtle – like the internal voice that questions whether you're good enough, ready enough or *worthy* enough to be in the room you've worked hard to enter.

That voice? That's imposter syndrome.

It's a form of self-doubt, rooted in the fear that sooner or later, someone will 'find you out'. That your wins were flukes. That your qualifications aren't enough. That you've somehow fooled everyone – and now, the jig is up.

We've heard this from mentees, clients, CEOs, creatives, professionals and even friends at the top of their game. The feeling that they've arrived somewhere they don't quite deserve to be.

Here's the truth: imposter syndrome doesn't mean you're unqualified. It means you're expanding.

The discomfort of growth often triggers these thoughts. You're in new territory, stretching into bigger rooms, new roles, fresh challenges. That unease is normal. But when left unchecked, it becomes a pattern that limits what you reach for next.

Where does it come from?

Psychologically, imposter syndrome is often linked to childhood experiences, cultural expectations or perfectionism. If you grew up being praised for high achievement, you may have developed a fear of not meeting those standards. If you were told to 'stay humble' or avoid 'showing off', you might now equate success with arrogance. And if you've ever been the only one who looked like you in the room – whether that's due to gender, race, background or education – then that sense of not belonging can deepen.

But none of that makes the fear accurate.

In fact, research from Dr Valerie Young, a leading expert on imposter syndrome, categorises it into five types:

- **The Perfectionist.** You focus on how things are done, and you're never satisfied.
- **The Expert.** You feel like you must know everything before you start.
- **The Soloist.** You believe asking for help means you're weak or unworthy.
- **The Natural Genius.** If something doesn't come easily, you feel inadequate.
- **The Superhuman.** You push yourself to excel in every role at once.

Most people fall into more than one category at different times in their lives. But the root is the same: a distorted belief about what success *should* look like and who you have to be to deserve it.

What can you do about it?

You don't need to wait until you *feel* confident to take action. In fact, taking action is often what *builds* confidence.

Here are some steps we recommend to reframe imposter syndrome and reduce the power it holds:

1 **Name it.** Call it what it is. The moment you say, 'Ah, this is imposter syndrome,' you create distance between the thought and your identity. It's not you. It's a temporary state of mind.
2 **Keep a wins file.** Start tracking your wins, big or small. Every great client review, promotion, sale, solution or moment of resilience. Keep screenshots, journal notes, feedback. Read it back when your brain tries to lie to you.
3 **Talk to someone who's been there.** Mentorship is a powerful antidote to imposter syndrome. Hearing from people who've succeeded in your field, despite the same

fears, reminds you that you're not alone and that self-doubt is normal but not permanent.

4 **Stop comparing drafts to highlights.** Especially in the age of social media, remember: people post the result, not the rejection emails, the failed launches or the late-night panic. Don't compare your process to their polish.

5 **Reframe the thought.** Instead of 'I don't belong here', try:
   - 'I earned my seat at the table.'
   - 'I'm learning, and that doesn't make me an imposter – it makes me committed.'
   - 'Confidence isn't a requirement. It's a result of showing up anyway.'

Our experience

Between us, we've written bestselling books, mentored thousands of individuals, built multiple businesses, stood on global stages, and advised top-tier organisations. And still there are moments where we feel it. That little voice that says, 'Are we doing enough?' 'Are we the right people for this room?'

But we've learned to speak back. To ground ourselves in truth, in action and in the results of showing up again and again, even when our minds aren't fully caught up with our reality.

If you've been there, too, know this: your fear of inadequacy is not a sign of unworthiness. It's a sign that you care. It means you're on the edge of something meaningful.

And what matters most is not how loudly doubt speaks but how firmly you act in spite of it.

Taking intentional steps forward

It's easy to assume that people who make bold moves must have everything figured out. That behind the decision is perfect certainty, flawless planning or unshakable confidence.

But that's rarely the truth.

Most of the time, the decision is made in the presence of fear – not in the absence of it. And the clarity doesn't come *before* the commitment – it often comes *because* of it.

That's certainly been true for us.

As we've planned our move to the UAE, there have been moments of excitement, anticipation and joy, but also moments of serious doubt, challenging logistics and complexity. There have been spreadsheets, late-night Google searches, long conversations, hard questions and honest reflection.

Because this isn't just a holiday or a project – it's a full transition of life.

We've had to break down this massive change into small, intentional steps. We didn't wake up one day and decide to move country. We planned, researched, tested, asked, learned and adjusted as we went. Every fear we had, we faced with action.

Here are some of the key steps we've taken that you can apply to your own journey – whether you're contemplating a career change, moving country, launching something new, or simply pushing yourself outside of your comfort zone.

Our steps to move through fear with purpose

1. GET CLEAR ON THE VISION

Before we even started figuring out the logistics, we got aligned on the dream. What did we actually want? What kind of life were we trying to build for ourselves and for our son? What would 'freedom' *feel* like, not just *look* like?

This clarity became our compass when the decisions got difficult.

Action for you: Write down what you truly want. Not the filtered, socially acceptable version. The real vision.

2. RESEARCH LIKE YOUR PEACE DEPENDS ON IT

We went deep. Schooling, healthcare, childcare, visas, cultural norms, climate, cost of living, location, business structures, communities. We didn't want to move blindly; we wanted to feel prepared, even if we couldn't control every outcome.

Action for you: If fear is rooted in the unknown, then get to know what you don't know. Make a research list. Get informed.

3. TEST THE WATERS

Before deciding to move permanently, we travelled. We stayed for extended periods in different places – spending time not as tourists but as temporary locals. We walked the streets, visited supermarkets, observed communities, tested daily life.

Action for you: Is there a way to 'test' your big move on a smaller scale? Can you shadow someone in that role? Trial a business offer? Spend a few weeks immersed in the new environment? Test-drive that car you have on your vision board?

4. BREAK IT DOWN

No major life-shift happens in one clean step. Ours involved:

- visa applications and paperwork
- property decisions
- budget and financial planning
- updating contracts and business structures
- planning for early parenting needs abroad
- connecting with a new support network

Each step, though imperfect, brought more clarity.

Action for you: List the next three *small* steps you can take towards your goal. Forget the full staircase. Just focus on the next few steps.

5. REVISIT YOUR 'WHY' OFTEN

There were moments when we questioned everything. But in those moments, we came back to our 'why'. Why did this matter to us? Why was the discomfort worth it? Why were we committed to seeing it through?

Action for you: Write your 'why' on a note. Stick it to your mirror, your laptop, your phone. Let it guide you when things feel uncertain.

This isn't about being brave. It's about being committed

We didn't move forward because we were fearless. We moved because we were clear and because we were willing to act in the presence of fear.

That's the lesson here.

You don't have to wait to feel bulletproof. You don't have to pretend the fear isn't there. You just need to get practical, get clear and move with purpose.

Because action is the great stabiliser. It grounds the fear. It gives you feedback. It builds evidence that you are capable, that you can adapt, that you're stronger than you think.

The fear might not leave straight away. But you'll start walking with it – until one day, you realise it's no longer leading.

Reflection exercise: Overcoming fear and doubt

Take some time to journal, voice-note or discuss your answers to the following. Let this be the moment you stop letting fear run the show.

1 **What fear has been holding me back, and where is it showing up?**

Identify it. Name it. Trace it to its source. Is it fear of rejection, failure, judgement, change?

_____

_____

_____

2 **What's the worst that could happen, and could I handle it?**

Play it out fully. Then ask: what's the best that could happen if I take this step?

_____

_____

_____

3 **Who or what in my circle fuels my fear or doubt, and who fuels my belief?**

Audit your environment. You don't have to cut people out, but you _do_ need to curate the voices that guide your growth.

_____

_____

_____

4 **Where have I succeeded before, even when I doubted myself?**

Let your past evidence fuel your future moves. You've done brave things before. This is no different.

_____

_____

_____

5 **What is one action I can take this week that moves me through fear?**

Something real. Something small. A phone call, an email, a conversation, a plan.

_____

_____

_____

Setting the stage for success

And finally, reflect on this . . .

- What if the fear never leaves – but you do it anyway?
- What if courage isn't the absence of fear, but your commitment to growth despite it?
- What if the version of you on the other side of this fear is the one you've been waiting for?

Fear doesn't need to disappear. It just needs to be demoted – from decision-maker to passenger.

It can come along for the ride, but you're the one behind the wheel now.

CHAPTER FIVE
Taking Consistent Action

The power of momentum

Let's be honest, motivation gets a lot of hype.

People talk about being 'inspired' or 'fired up' to do something. They wait for the perfect mood to strike. The right quote. The sunny morning. The ideal headspace. But the truth is, **motivation is fleeting. It comes and goes.**

What really matters – what really builds the life you want – is **consistency.**

Because consistent action is what separates those who dream from those who deliver.

I (Byron) have met thousands of people through our mentoring programmes, courses and events. Many of them have brilliant ideas. Many of them have the vision. But the ones who build something truly life-changing? They're not necessarily the most talented, the most connected or the loudest in the room.

They're the ones who do the work, even when they don't feel like it.

Even when no one's watching.
Even when it's hard.
Even when it's boring.

That's what this chapter is about.

It's about learning how to build consistent habits that support your vision. It's about moving through the days when fear creeps back in, or when life gets noisy, or when your goal starts to feel heavy instead of exciting. It's about creating rhythm, resilience and routine around your ambition.

Because manifestation without consistent action is like trying to grow a garden without ever watering it.

You don't need explosive effort once in a while; you need purposeful movement every day.

Why consistency is the real secret sauce

If there's one thing I've learned over the last fifteen years of building businesses, mentoring, consulting and strategising – it's this:

Consistency is the real game-changer.

Not the hype. Not the headlines. Not the viral moments.

It's the boring stuff. The behind-the-scenes. The unsexy repetition that most people skip.

You see, most people think success looks like fireworks. And sometimes it does. But the truth is, the real foundations of business – and life – are built in the quiet, in the discipline, in the days when no one is clapping.

And I can say that with confidence because I've lived it.

Back when I was just starting out in business – in my early twenties, still green to the game – I made a decision that would shape everything: I was going to invest in my personal development, no matter what. Even when the business wasn't thriving. Even when it felt uncomfortable. Even when the budget said, 'Don't do it.'

And I didn't just go alone – I brought my team with me. Not because it was fashionable. Not because everyone was doing it. But because I understood, even then, that knowledge compounds. That exposure to new ways of thinking was essential. And that no one builds a powerful business or brand without becoming someone who can handle it.

There were days I'd sit in those rooms – training courses, business development workshops, sales seminars – feeling like I was the youngest in the room, or the least experienced. But I kept showing up. I kept listening. I kept asking questions.

Fast-forward to now, and I've invested well over six figures in my personal development. Courses. Mentorship. Masterminds. Travel. Industry consultants. Advisors. Strategy sessions. Some of them changed my life. Others were just okay. But all of them taught me something.

And here's what most people don't realise: as the businesses grow, so do the stakes – and so must the investment.

Now, as our companies scale, my personal development budget has increased. Not because I have to keep up appearances, but because *I'm still growing*. Still evolving. Still sharpening my ability to see opportunities, navigate challenges and lead at a high level. I don't just go to training for the sake of it; I go because the next level of impact demands a better version of me.

But it's not just about me.

We continue to send our team to the courses, events and training that we believe will elevate their knowledge, their confidence and their contribution to the business. Why? Because we believe in building people. And when those people eventually move on – and some do – they leave better, sharper and more employable than when they joined us. That matters to us.

We don't just build businesses. We build people

That consistency – of learning, investing, developing – has been the real secret. It's not the projects that went viral. It's not the one big win. It's the hours no one sees.

Even now, when I want to move into a new industry, launch a new vertical or scale an idea from six to seven figures, I do what I've always done. I find the people who've done it. I study the model. I invest in the learning. I accelerate the journey with focus.

And look, your version of that might be different:

It might be buying this book.
It might be attending one of our live online events.
**It might be joining one of our mentoring programmes
or enrolling in our in-person academy.**

It might be reading for 20 minutes a day or listening to a podcast while you're on the school run.

But make no mistake: consistency in your development is not optional. It's your leverage.

How to build momentum (even when you don't feel like it)

Let me tell you something straight: **you're not going to feel like it every day**.

There are going to be mornings where you question why you started. Days where the to-do list feels overwhelming. Moments where progress feels so slow, it would be easier to quit than push.

And if you're building something from scratch – or scaling something that demands more of you – that feeling is even more real.

But here's the truth I learned the hard way, back when I was running my business as a sole trader and barely scraping through month to month:

Discipline beats motivation. Every single time.

Motivation is great. It's that buzz you get when you hear a great talk, attend an event, or watch someone else winning. But what happens when that feeling wears off? What happens when you're tired, or things get quiet, or you're not getting the recognition you hoped for?

That's when consistency steps in. That's when routine becomes your safety net. And that's when momentum – real, lasting momentum – is built.

Momentum isn't magic. It's made

Momentum is not about speed. It's about direction. It's about taking small, repeatable actions that stack up over time.

Back in the early days, I didn't always know what I was doing. I didn't have access to big budgets or teams. But I did have structure. I created systems. I set targets. I blocked out time for follow-ups, prospecting, self-study, networking.

Even when there wasn't a big result, I stayed in motion. Because I knew that consistency builds credibility. And credibility builds opportunity.

It's like going to the gym. You don't see results on day one. Or week one. But you keep showing up. You lift. You sweat. You stretch. Then, suddenly, your body starts changing and everyone wants to know your secret.

The secret? You kept going when no one was clapping.

My systems for staying consistent

Here's how I keep things moving now, even when I'm not in the mood. Even with businesses, staff, family life and international plans all running at once.

1. LOCK IN YOUR NON-NEGOTIABLES

I've got a few things I do *no matter what*. It might be reviewing financials every Friday. Catching up with my business development team on Mondays. Blocking time to work on growth opportunities weekly. These don't move. They're set in stone.

That's how you create structure – because when the chaos comes (and it will), you've already built in the core routines to carry you through.

2. TIME-BOX YOUR FOCUS

Distractions are everywhere. Your phone. Your inbox. People pulling you in ten different directions.

When I've got something that needs focus – whether it's a new business proposal or planning for a project – I give it a fixed window. No multitasking. No noise. Just deep work.

Even 45 minutes of focused time can move the needle more than three hours of scattered effort.

3. TRACK, DON'T GUESS

I track what matters. Revenue. Enquiries. Conversion rates. Pipeline value. If you don't track it, you can't improve it. And you can't build momentum on vibes alone.

This is how you stay consistent – **by knowing where you are and where you're going**.

4. BREAK IT DOWN

Big projects overwhelm people because they try to do everything at once. I break everything into phases. A launch might have 30 steps, but if today's focus is just on step two, I'm winning.

Clarity reduces resistance.

5. STAY ACCOUNTABLE

In the early days, I was accountable to myself and my goals. Now, I'm accountable to my team, my family, my legacy. And I still check in with mentors and peers.

If you're struggling with consistency, ask yourself: **who are you reporting to?** Not in a policing way, but in a growth-focused, 'I'm serious about this' kind of way.

You don't need to feel it – you just need to do it

Some days, I'm tired. Some days, I'm juggling back-to-back strategy calls. Some days, our son wakes up at 5 a.m. and the whole day shifts. But I still find a way to show up.

Not because I'm a robot. But because I've trained myself to do what needs to be done – whether I feel like it or not.

That's how you build greatness. That's how you lead. That's how you win.

Staying accountable without burning out

Let's get something clear – **accountability is not about pressure. It's about structure.**

The people who keep showing up and winning in life, business and relationships aren't always operating at 100 percent. They're not superhuman. They just have systems around them that stop them from drifting too far off course.

And if there's one thing I've learned over the years – from being a sole trader working alone, to running multiple teams across different industries – it's that **you can't grow what you can't manage, and you can't manage what you don't measure**.

What accountability really means

For a lot of people, the word 'accountability' feels like punishment. Like being back at school and waiting to be told off. But that's not how I see it.

To me, accountability is alignment with your future self. It's checking in – not to judge yourself, but to remind yourself what you're building, why it matters, and whether your actions are helping or hindering.

And yes, you can hold yourself accountable. But let's be honest – self-discipline has its limits, especially when life gets full. That's why systems and people matter.

Three levels of accountability that work

1. SELF-ACCOUNTABILITY (YOUR INNER SCORECARD)

What do you hold yourself to? Are you meeting your own standards, or just reacting to life as it comes?

I keep a personal dashboard of my key priorities – projects, revenue targets, personal habits. If something's slipping, I know. I don't wait for the consequences to show up – I adjust.

2. TEAM OR PEER ACCOUNTABILITY (EXTERNAL CHECK-INS)

Whether it's a business partner, a coach or a trusted team member, you need someone to reflect on progress with. Someone who'll ask, 'Have you done it?' or 'Is that still the goal?' – without judgement but with honesty.

In our companies, I don't just delegate, I stay connected. If someone needs direction or clarity, we handle it early. That's how we avoid spirals.

3. STRUCTURAL ACCOUNTABILITY (SYSTEMS THAT NUDGE YOU)

This is where most people fall off – because it's not glamorous.

I'm talking scheduled reviews. KPI trackers. Budget check-ins. Content calendars. Project dashboards. These aren't restrictive – they're freeing. Because they reduce decision fatigue. You don't have to wake up and reinvent the wheel; you just follow the system.

Burnout: The enemy of consistency

Let's be real: **burnout isn't just 'being a bit tired'.**

It's a full-body, full-mind breakdown of energy, clarity and motivation. It's what happens when you've been operating at full tilt for too long without rest, support or recalibration. And whether you're an entrepreneur, a parent, a professional or all three at once, it can hit hard and derail everything.

Burnout doesn't usually show up as one dramatic collapse. It's sneaky. It builds slowly. You stop sleeping well. You struggle to focus. You start resenting the very work you once loved. You feel detached. Easily irritable. Constantly behind. But you keep pushing, because the world has conditioned us to believe that stopping – even briefly – means failure.

But burnout isn't a badge of honour. It's a warning light. A signal that something needs to shift before your vision starts costing you more than it gives.

And this is not just theory: it happens to the best in the game.

Real life: Whitney Wolfe Herd and the burnout break

Take Whitney Wolfe Herd, founder of Bumble. She led one of the most culturally disruptive companies of the past decade, redefining online dating by giving women the first move. But success at scale came with real pressure.

By 2021, Bumble had grown into a global tech brand, and Wolfe Herd had just taken the company public, becoming the youngest woman in history to lead a firm to IPO. But behind the scenes, she and her team were running on fumes. Endless meetings. Back-to-back product rollouts. Media attention. A pandemic. Remote working challenges.

Wolfe Herd recognised the signs early – not just in herself, but in her entire workforce.

So what did she do?

She shut the company down for a full week. All 700-plus employees were given paid time off to rest and recover. No meetings. No Slack messages. No performance reviews. Just time to reset.

She didn't wait until the entire company cracked – she acted at the tipping point.

As Clare O'Connor, Bumble's head of editorial, put it at the time: 'Whitney correctly intuited our collective burnout.'[1]

That move wasn't just progressive, it was powerful. It sent a message to the tech world and beyond that protecting your people *is* protecting your business.

Burnout is personal – and it's universal

On a different level, Arianna Huffington – another high-profile founder – faced her own reckoning when she collapsed in her office from exhaustion, breaking her cheekbone on the way down. That moment led her to re-evaluate everything she thought she knew about productivity. She later founded Thrive Global to champion wellbeing over burnout culture.

And then there's Prince Harry, who's opened up about emotional burnout in the face of intense public scrutiny and personal trauma. He shared how years of suppressing his mental health needs eventually led to burnout that impacted his family, work and wellbeing, forcing him to seek help and change direction.

These stories might seem far removed from your day-to-day life, but the root issue is the same: **the relentless pressure to keep going, even when your body, mind and soul are asking you to slow down.**

What burnout looked like for me

I've felt it, too.

There were years in my business when the calendar was full, the contracts were coming in, and it looked like everything was working. But I was fried. I wasn't eating properly. I was sleeping four or five hours a night. I was saying yes to everything. My mind never stopped spinning.

And here's the kicker: I told myself it was necessary. That being in survival mode was just part of the game.

But it wasn't.

It was a pattern I had to unlearn. Because I realised I was building something that looked successful but was draining the person running it.

That's when I started building real boundaries, creating better systems, and letting go of the guilt around rest.

Recognise the signs. Reclaim the pace

Here are some signs you might be facing burnout, even if you're high-functioning on the outside:

- You wake up already tired.
- You feel emotionally numb, even during wins.
- You snap at minor frustrations.
- You struggle to feel motivated by things you used to enjoy.
- You dread your inbox or feel overwhelmed before the day even starts.
- You constantly feel 'behind', even when you're making progress.

If any of these resonate, it's time to take stock. Not just to avoid crashing, but to protect the version of you who's here to lead and thrive.

Success is not meant to come at the cost of your wellbeing. If you're building something great, it should nourish you, not destroy you.

Burnout isn't a sign of strength. It's a sign of misalignment.

How I stay grounded (without falling behind)

1 **I build in buffers.** Every project has breathing room. I don't stack my days to the edge. I leave space to think, redirect or simply breathe.
2 **I don't do everything myself.** Delegation isn't a weakness. It's leadership. The bigger the vision, the more support you'll need.
3 **I protect recovery time.** Rest is part of performance. Whether it's a walk with my son, time with Bianca, watching football or unplugged hours in the gym, I respect recovery as much as the work.
4 **I work in seasons.** Some seasons are intense – launching something new, closing deals, restructuring teams. But other seasons are intentionally slower. This rhythm keeps the engine running without burning out the motor.

What this means for you

If you're serious about manifesting your goals, you need both pace and protection:

- Build a system that works for your life.
- Identify the accountability you need and make it visible.
- Rest without guilt, and work without chaos.
- Make your consistency *sustainable*, not stressful.

Because anyone can sprint for a week. But it's the ones who can run *smart* over the long term who cross finish lines again and again.

Aligning action with your goals

Consistency is powerful. But **consistency in the wrong direction** is just wasted effort.

We've all heard the phrase 'hard work pays off', and, for the most part, that's true. But here's what they don't often tell you – **hard work that isn't aligned with your actual goal doesn't just wear you out, it slows you down.**

Because being busy isn't the same as being effective.

Let me share a personal example that really hit this home for me.

The wake-up call: Don't be a busy fool

There was a point in my journey where my property services business was thriving – on paper. We had a full diary. Assessors were booked solid. The team was running from job to job. Phones were ringing. On the surface, everything looked like progress.

But here's the kicker: the bank account didn't reflect it.

And I remember sitting down with Bianca's dad, a fellow entrepreneur, to talk things through. We were reflecting on how hard we were all working, and I must have said something along the lines of: 'Business is going great – we're fully booked.'

He paused, looked at me, and said: **'Don't be a busy fool.'**

That hit me like a brick. Because he was right.

We were moving, but we weren't moving forward. We had action, but no alignment. The goals were there – growth, sustainability, profitability – but the systems, pricing and strategy didn't reflect those goals. We were doing the *work*, but not the *right* work.

From that moment on, I made a conscious decision to be more strategic. To check whether the daily grind was building towards the bigger vision or just keeping us occupied.

Busy ≠ productive. Movement ≠ progress

And this doesn't just apply to business owners. I've seen it with career professionals, too. You can spend years in a role – doing what's asked

78

of you, ticking boxes, working overtime – and still not be any closer to the promotion, the pay rise or the role you really want.

Why? Because you're not moving with intention. You're moving out of habit. And that habit can become a trap.

That's what aligning your action to your goals is really about. It's not just about effort, it's about direction.

It's about asking yourself: **'Is what I'm doing right now bringing me closer to the life I'm building?'**

If the answer is no – or, worse, 'I don't know' – then it's time to pause, recalibrate and get clear.

What aligned action looks like

Aligned action is deliberate. It's designed. It's connected to a bigger picture. Here's what that means in practice:

1 **Your diary reflects your priorities.** If your calendar is full but none of the items relate to your long-term goals, you're going to hit a wall. Whether it means carving out time for business strategy, networking, health or personal growth, your goals need to have a place in your week, not just your mind.

2 **Your tasks have a 'why'.** Before starting something, ask: why am I doing this? If the answer is 'in order to stay afloat' or 'because I've always done it', that's not good enough.

3 **Your results are measurable.** If you're working hard but can't see progress – more leads, higher income, improved systems, better health – it's time to reassess. You can't align with what you don't define.

4 **You're not afraid to adjust.** Sometimes the bravest move is pivoting. Saying, 'This isn't working.' Or, 'We need to raise prices.' Or, 'It's time to bring in help.' Misalignment is not failure – it's a chance to course-correct.

From hectic to high-performance

After that moment with Bianca's dad, I went back to the business and started making some changes:

- We reviewed our pricing structure.
- We looked at where we were losing time and where our profit margins were thin.
- We optimised routes, processes and client touchpoints.
- We raised the standard – not just of the service, but of the strategy behind it.
- And guess what? The diary stayed full but, this time, the numbers matched the effort.

The takeaway

You don't need to be busy. You need to be *effective*.

Aligned action means doing what matters. What moves the needle. What supports the lifestyle, legacy and leadership you're working towards – not just what fills your day.

So before you race to tick off another task, ask yourself: **'Is this action aligned with where I'm going – or just keeping me from feeling guilty?'**

Consistent action across the Five Principles

One of the best pieces of advice I can give anyone is this: **consistency isn't just for your business or your job title; it needs to be applied across your whole life.**

Why? Because success isn't siloed. You might be thriving financially, but burning out physically. You might be advancing in your career, but neglecting your family or your health. And eventually, the cracks will show.

That's why Bianca and I always bring things back to the Five Principles – career, entrepreneurship, family and relationships, self and health. These are the core areas where most of our dreams live, and if you want to manifest anything meaningful, you need to be taking consistent, aligned action in each.

Let's break this down.

1. CAREER

If you're in a job or building a corporate career, consistent action is what builds reputation, opportunity and progression.

It's the follow-through after you've said, 'I want to lead,' or 'I'm aiming for promotion.' It's how you show up every day, not just when the appraisal meeting is around the corner.

Aligned actions in this principle might look like:

- booking regular one-to-ones with your line manager to discuss development
- upskilling intentionally – learning the things that will get you into the next role
- raising your visibility at work (volunteering for key projects, sharing wins)
- tracking your performance so that when the opportunity arises, you're ready

2. ENTREPRENEURSHIP

This one's personal. I've been in business since 2003 and one of the biggest things I've learned is that **a great idea without consistent action is just an expensive hobby.**

So many entrepreneurs live in reactive mode – just trying to survive the week. But if you want to build something that scales, that supports you and your team, then you need to make consistency non-negotiable.

Aligned actions in this principle might look like:

- reviewing your numbers weekly – not just revenue, but profit, pipeline and performance
- building repeatable systems so you don't reinvent the wheel with every client

- booking in business development activity weekly, not just when you're quiet
- investing in your own growth – even when money's tight, even when it's not glamorous

3. FAMILY AND RELATIONSHIPS

This is a big one for me, especially now that Bianca and I are raising our son. We don't just want to build successful businesses; we want to build a strong home. A safe, joyful, connected environment.

But you can't manifest that kind of family life with good intentions alone. It requires time. Energy. Planning. And, yes, consistency.

Aligned actions in this principle might look like:

- creating dedicated, phone-free family time every day, even if it's just 30 minutes
- checking in with your partner intentionally, not just when things feel off
- planning ahead so you're present for the moments that matter (not reacting at the last minute)
- building a home rhythm that supports everyone's growth, not just that of the adults

4. SELF

This one often gets left behind, but, trust me, it's the foundation.

You are the vessel through which every goal, vision and legacy will flow. If you're depleted, insecure or stuck, everything else will suffer. Your self-consistency builds self-trust – and, from there, anything is possible.

Aligned actions in this principle might look like:

- having morning or evening rituals that keep you grounded and focused
- speaking to yourself with respect and cutting the negative self-talk
- making space for personal goals, not just business or family ones
- investing in your own therapy, coaching or creative passions

5. HEALTH

This isn't just about having abs or running marathons (unless that's your thing). It's about having the energy, clarity and longevity to carry your dreams into the future.

When I'm not taking care of my health, I feel it in every area. Business. Relationships. Mood. Focus. That's why I treat my health habits with the same respect I give to financial strategy or team leadership.

Aligned actions in this principle might look like:

- moving daily – even if it's just a walk or stretch
- eating to fuel yourself, not just to get through the day
- hydrating, sleeping, unplugging – simple but game-changing
- addressing small issues early, before they become big ones

Consistency across the board

The key to manifested action is understanding that all five of these principles work together. You can't be wildly consistent in one and totally neglect the others – not if you want your success to be sustainable.

So start where you are. Choose one principle. Then ask: 'What would consistent action look like here, and how can I make that a habit?'

When you align your action across your life – not just in one lane – you don't just achieve your goals. **You become the kind of person who can sustain them.**

Consistency isn't glamorous. It won't always make headlines.

But it is the one thing, above all, that separates those who wish for success from those who *create* it.

Every chapter of your life will require something different from you. But if you want to build something meaningful – whether it's a business, a career, a relationship or a legacy – you need to make action a daily habit, not just an occasional burst.

Because manifestation without action is fantasy.

And action without consistency is just chaos.

You don't need to be perfect. You don't need to hustle until you burn out. But you *do* need to stay in motion – with intention, structure and clarity.

Whether you're trying to grow a business, break into a new career, improve your health or deepen your relationships, **consistency is your compound interest.**

It builds quietly. Then it builds quickly. And suddenly, you realise you've become the version of yourself you used to imagine.

Reflection exercise: Taking consistent action

Take some time to sit with the questions below. Use them to ground your intentions, sharpen your focus, and create the consistency you need to keep moving forward.

1 **Where am I confusing busyness with progress?** Am I filling time, or truly building something? Which daily tasks are truly aligned with my bigger goals?

_____

_____

_____

2 **What systems or routines would help me show up more consistently?** This could be a morning ritual, a weekly planning session or even a ten-minute daily review. What will anchor your habits?

_____

_____

_____

3 **Who or what am I accountable to?** Do I have someone –
   or something – that helps keep me aligned? If not, what kind
   of accountability system could support me?

   _____

   _____

   _____

4 **What signs of burnout have I been ignoring?** Where
   do I need to slow down, delegate or say no in order to sustain my energy and mental clarity?

   _____

   _____

   _____

5 **How can I apply consistent action across the Five
   Principles of my life?** Career. Entrepreneurship. Family
   and relationships. Self. Health. Where am I showing up well,
   and where have I been coasting?

   _____

   _____

   _____

Your action plan: Start small, stay strong

Here are five practical steps to embed consistency into your routine this week:

1 **Choose one goal you want to prioritise.** Write it down in detail.

_____

_____

_____

2 **List three small actions that would move you closer to that goal, then schedule them.**

_____

_____

_____

3 **Find one person you can check in with regularly about your progress.** Write their name here and how often will you check in with them.

_____

_____

_____

4 **Audit your time.** What are you doing daily that doesn't support your growth?

_____

_____

_____

5 **Celebrate one win this week – no matter how small.**
Progress deserves recognition. Write down the details here.

_____

_____

_____

Setting the stage for success

Remember, you're not aiming for perfection. You're aiming for
progress you can repeat.

Because it's not what you do once that transforms your life –
it's what you do over and over again.

The consistency of your action is what gives power to your
vision. So keep showing up.

You've got this.

CHAPTER SIX
Building Resilience

The bounce-back blueprint

Life is full of detours. Unexpected turns. Roadblocks. Dead ends.

Sometimes the sat nav reroutes, and sometimes you find yourself staring at a brick wall thinking, 'How did I get here – and how do I move forward?'

But here's the thing – **resilience isn't about avoiding the detour. It's about learning to navigate through it, and bounce back better.**

One of the biggest bounce-backs I (Bianca) have had to master in recent years hasn't been a dramatic business failure or personal disaster. It's been the process of returning to work after having my son.

Now, I know when people talk about 'bouncing back' after birth, it usually refers to getting your body back. Let me stop you right there – this isn't *that* kind of chapter. My bounce-back wasn't about waistlines or wardrobes; it was about *work*. About stepping back into a world that moves fast and doesn't always wait for you to catch your breath.

As an entrepreneur, there's no HR department lining up a structured 12-month maternity leave. There's no out-of-office that works on staff, consultants or clients who 'just have a quick question' three weeks after you've given birth.

I still remember it vividly. March – International Women's Month – was always a packed time in my calendar. And, in 2024, I delivered my final keynote for a FTSE 100 company, standing on stage nine months pregnant in the UK's largest exhibition venue. A room filled with career women. I gave that talk knowing it was my last for a while. I was 37 weeks along, and figured I had time to nest, rest and maybe even binge-watch Netflix. You know, the calm before the storm.

What actually happened? One week later, I went in for a routine scan.

The obstetrician looked up from the screen and said, 'Bianca, baby hasn't grown enough this week. We think it's time to bring him/her into the world.'

It was Wednesday. By Saturday, I was giving birth.

Friday night, we stayed in central London – our final night as a couple. Saturday evening, two became three. And my life as I knew it changed for ever.

A new kind of resilience

The year that followed taught me a new kind of resilience.

Not just as a woman, but as a wife, a mother and a founder.

There's no handbook for how to juggle nap schedules, feeding routines and client deadlines – especially when you're also trying to protect your mental wellbeing, recover from birth and nurture a tiny human who depends on you for literally everything.

I had glorious months immersed in baby sensory classes, long pram walks, mummy-and-baby yoga, giggles, 3 a.m. feeds, and – alongside my husband – figuring out this thing called parenting, learning together how to keep our son, Ethan, alive and thriving.

But I also had a decision to make: would I let the fear of falling behind stop me, or would I trust the foundation I'd already laid?

I chose to manifest a new vision. I wasn't aiming to return to where I was. I was building something *beyond* that.

So I put my trust in what I'd created before Ethan arrived:

- a brand that spoke for itself
- a personal brand profile rooted in value and consistency
- a team equipped to keep the engine running – my SEO, LinkedIn, outreach and sales didn't stop just because I wasn't visible
- a plan, not just for surviving maternity, but for returning *stronger*

And then, I set my sights on a new goal: March 2025 – International Women's Month – would be my biggest speaking season yet (while returning to work part-time).

I visualised myself back on stage. Not just as the woman I was before birth, but as someone evolved. Expanded. Emboldened.

From manifestation to momentum

And here's the beautiful part: it happened.

In March 2025, I delivered nine speaking engagements across prestigious brands – Amazon, Barclays, CMS LLP, MONY Group and more. I travelled across the UK. My diary was full again for 2025, with speaking clients, consulting work and mentoring. The bounce-back was in full effect – not because I forced it, but because I aligned intention with action.

Because I allowed myself to visualise a successful return while accepting that it wouldn't look exactly like before. And because I didn't try to do it all – I empowered my team, leaned into systems and let consistency carry me when energy was low.

Resilience isn't a personality trait, it's a practice

This chapter is for anyone who's ever had to start again.

For those navigating a comeback, recovering from disappointment or questioning whether you can still create the life you dream of.

Resilience isn't just grit or toughness.

It's hope in motion.
It's the belief that your story isn't over.
It's the ability to move forward, one step at a time – even
with the scars, the doubts and the new responsibilities
in tow.

And if I can do it – with milk stains on my top and 15 minutes of sleep – then so can you.

What resilience really looks like

When people picture resilience, they often imagine someone charging forward, head held high, with a bulletproof mindset and a heart full of fire. They think resilience means powering through pain, brushing off rejection and keeping a stiff upper lip – no matter what life throws at you.

But let me be honest: real resilience doesn't always look fierce or fearless. Sometimes, resilience looks like holding yourself together with a messy bun, a lukewarm coffee and a deep breath you've had to take six times already this morning.

Sometimes it's calm. Sometimes it's chaotic. Sometimes it's just showing up.

Resilience is not about always being okay. It's about choosing to move anyway, even when you're not.

We've been sold this idea that resilience means being 'strong'. But what does strong really mean? Stoic? Silent? Unbothered? That version of strength often isolates people, especially women. Especially leaders. Especially anyone who feels like they can't afford to have an off day.

Let's drop the performance.

True resilience is *quietly radical*. It's staying soft while life tries to harden you. It's saying, 'I'm not giving up,' even while tears are streaming down your face. It's falling apart . . . and then pulling yourself back together, piece by piece, without waiting for permission or applause.

Resilience in real life (not just on Instagram)

I've seen what real resilience looks like – not on a filtered feed, but in real life.

It's the new mother juggling three feeds a night, still turning up to her side hustle each morning.
It's the entrepreneur relaunching their business after their first idea flopped and their bank account dried up.
It's the career professional who gets passed over for a promotion, feels the sting of it, and still shows up to the next meeting with a notebook, a plan and grace.

I've worked with women who've battled imposter syndrome, health scares, lay-offs, toxic workplaces, break-ups, grief . . . and still found a way to *keep building*. Not because they're invincible, but because they knew their vision was still worth pursuing.

The myth of the 'bounce-back'

We love a good comeback story, don't we? But what we don't talk about enough is how long the bounce-back takes. And how many silent, lonely, unglamorous steps it's made up of.

There's no overnight return. No neat little arc.

There's just *the decision* – sometimes made daily – to keep going.

And that is resilience: the quiet decision to show up again.

Resilience doesn't mean pushing through at any cost. It means adapting, evolving and protecting your energy as you grow. Sometimes it means resting. Sometimes it means shifting the goal. Sometimes it means asking for help.

It's not about doing it all. It's about doing what matters, and doing it in a way that allows you to keep going.

The science of setbacks

Let's get into the *why* behind what we feel.

It's one thing to say, 'Keep going.' It's another to understand why our brains and bodies sometimes make that feel nearly impossible. When we face a setback – a rejection, a failure, a harsh piece of feedback, or even just the sting of unmet expectations – our nervous system doesn't necessarily see it as a minor inconvenience.

It sees it as a threat.

WHAT HAPPENS IN YOUR BRAIN DURING A SETBACK

When we experience failure or emotional pain, the brain lights up in very similar regions to those that light up when we experience

93

physical pain. That's right: your brain doesn't really distinguish between heartbreak and a paper cut.

Specifically, the anterior cingulate cortex and the insula cortex are activated during both social rejection and physical pain. This is why a bad review or being excluded from an opportunity can feel like a literal punch to the gut.

When this happens, the amygdala (your brain's fear centre) kicks into high gear. It triggers a fight, flight, freeze or fawn response – even if all that's happened is a tough meeting or a missed deadline.

Your body floods with **cortisol**, the stress hormone, and if that isn't balanced by recovery time or support, it can linger – leading to long-term fatigue, brain fog and emotional reactivity. Sound familiar?

THE ROLE OF THE GROWTH MINDSET

Here's where the good news comes in: your brain is not fixed.

Thanks to neuroplasticity, we now know that the brain can change – adapt, grow and rewire itself based on how we respond to experiences.

Psychologist Dr Carol Dweck introduced the idea of a *growth mindset* versus a *fixed mindset*. People with a fixed mindset believe their abilities are static – you're either good at something or you're not. So when they fail, they take it personally. It confirms their fear that they weren't good enough in the first place.

People with a *growth mindset*, on the other hand, see challenges as opportunities. They view setbacks as feedback – not as a reflection of their worth but as a stepping stone to mastery.

The question is no longer 'Did I fail?' but 'What can I learn from this?'

And that shift is everything.

It's not about pretending everything is fine. It's about training your brain to stay curious instead of collapsing. It's about asking *why?* instead of *why me?*

REWIRING FOR RESILIENCE

Think of your brain like a set of walking trails. The more often you travel one path (e.g. self-doubt, catastrophising), the more worn it becomes. But if you start walking a different route – *reframing the narrative, practising self-compassion, seeking solutions* – those new pathways strengthen over time.

Eventually, the response becomes automatic.

That's not magic. That's science.

And it means you can learn to respond to setbacks in a way that builds you rather than breaking you.

As fitness expert Lewis Paris often reminds me, 'Mental resilience is a muscle – and like any other muscle, it gets stronger when you put it under pressure.' Lewis, whose work in longevity and elite performance has impacted leaders, athletes and professionals across industries, believes that the gym is one of the most underrated places in which to build your mindset. 'There's something powerful that happens when you push your body beyond what it thought it could do,' he told me. 'If you can lift that weight, run that distance, finish that final round, you start to realise that maybe you *can* do hard things in life, too.'

That crossover isn't just anecdotal. Research shared in *Frontiers in Psychology* shows that strength-training improves not only physical capacity but also executive function, stress tolerance and emotional regulation.[1] It's as if every rep isn't just sculpting your body; it's rewiring your brain to associate pressure with possibility, not panic.

Celebrities and leaders alike lean on this principle. Think Dwayne 'The Rock' Johnson, who's long spoken about using his 4 a.m. workouts not just for fitness but as a daily anchor for discipline, focus and mental clarity. Michelle Obama famously prioritised her gym sessions during her time in the White House – not for aesthetics, but for sanity. Even Oprah Winfrey has said her morning exercise routine helps her 'reset mentally' and reclaim control over her day.

So, is strength-training a secret superhero hack for resilience?

It just might be. Not because lifting weights solves every problem, but because it helps you show up to those problems with a different energy.

And, sometimes, that shift is everything.

Building resilience – the everyday toolkit

Resilience isn't something you wake up with one day: 'Oh look, I'm resilient now.'

It's built. Intentionally. Bit by bit. Thought by thought. Decision by decision.

And the beauty of it is, you don't need a crisis to build resilience. You can start practising in the everyday moments. The annoying ones. The awkward ones. The ones where things just don't quite go to plan.

Here's a toolkit I've built over the years – shaped by personal trial and error, lessons from mentors and clients, and watching some truly remarkable people find their bounce-back rhythm, even when the odds weren't in their favour.

1. REFRAME THE CHALLENGE

Resilient people don't avoid difficulty, they reinterpret it.

That doesn't mean sugar-coating hardship. It means zooming out and asking: what could this teach me? Where is the growth hiding here?

Take the entrepreneur whose launch flopped – not once but twice. Instead of labelling herself a failure, she looked at her audience data, refined her messaging and relaunched with a smaller, more engaged community. She hit her sales target on the third go – not because she didn't fall, but because she fell *forward*.

And I've seen it in careers, too. One of my coaching clients was made redundant during a restructure. She spiralled at first, as many would. But within two weeks, we'd reframed her situation as a chance to *pivot*. She signed up for a course, activated her network, and within three months had landed a role with better pay and more flexibility.

Reframing is a mental workout. But it gets easier with practice.

2. PRACTISE SELF-COMPASSION

This one is huge, especially for high performers. We're brilliant at showing compassion to others, but when it comes to ourselves? Brutal.

Talk to yourself like you would a friend.

If your friend made a mistake or missed a goal, would you say, 'You're a disaster'? No – you'd say, 'That was tough. But you're not defined by this. What do you want to do next?'

Try saying it to yourself.

One stay-at-home mum I worked with felt like she'd 'lost herself' after two years out of the workplace. But what she was really missing was compassion – for what she'd achieved, how she'd held her family together, and the skills she'd gained along the way. Once we reframed her experience as valuable, her confidence returned – and so did her career trajectory.

Self-compassion isn't soft. It's *strong*. Because it allows you to fail forward, without losing your sense of worth.

3. ASK FOR HELP (BEFORE YOU'RE DROWNING)

This might be the hardest one of all.

We live in a world that idolises independence. But resilience doesn't mean doing it all yourself. It means **knowing when and where to lean on others**.

Support systems look different for everyone:

- a fellow business-owner who checks in weekly
- a therapist or coach who helps you process and plan
- a partner who knows when to step in and take the reins
- a parent WhatsApp group that shares tips, meal hacks and moral support

Even a well-timed podcast or book can act as a form of emotional scaffolding.

You are not weak for needing help. You are wise for *using* help.

4. CELEBRATE SMALL COMEBACKS

We wait too long to celebrate. We wait for the full recovery, the six-figure launch, the dream promotion, the clean bill of health.

But resilience lives in the *small* wins:

- Getting out of bed on a hard day? That's a win.
- Posting on LinkedIn again after a break? Win.

- Pitching yourself to a new client after a 'no'? Win.
- Making it through the week with a teething baby, a tired brain and your sanity intact? Massive win.

One of my favourite rituals with clients is creating a 'Resilience Resume' – a list of every time they've come back from something difficult. It shifts the focus from what's missing to what's already within them. Try it.

5. JOURNAL IT OUT (EVEN IF IT'S SCRAPPY)

You don't need to be a writer to journal. You just need to feel something.

Use your journal as a space to:

- dump the emotion that's clogging your thoughts
- make sense of a situation that's thrown you off course
- track patterns – wins – triggers – progress
- remind yourself of what you've survived and what you're aiming for

Even five minutes before bed can give you a mental reset and a moment to remember: *you're still here, still growing, still moving forward.*

Stress, pressure and the mental load

Let's talk about the *weight* we carry.

Not just the meetings, the deadlines or the school drop-offs, but the *mental spreadsheets*, the tabs open in our brains, the emotional load we never quite switch off.

Because let's be honest: in today's world, most of us are wearing more hats than our heads were designed to hold.

The juggle is real

I'm not just a founder. I'm also an author. A mother. A wife. A daughter. A friend. A mentor. A speaker. A strategist. A business owner.

And every single one of those roles carries its own to-do list, emotional register and expectations – many of which are invisible.

And this isn't just a conversation about women. My husband, Byron, carries just as many hats. During the early days of parenting, while I was adjusting to life with our newborn, he was sharing the night shifts, making sure the businesses kept growing and supporting *me* through the biggest identity shift I've ever experienced.

We were both showing up, just in different lanes.

That's the reality of modern life. No matter your gender or job title – *everyone's carrying something.*

The hidden weight: Mental and emotional load

Sometimes the stress we feel isn't about the workload itself.

It's about everything we carry *in our heads*:

- remembering everyone's birthdays
- being the default decision-maker
- prepping the strategy for Monday while trying to soothe a teething toddler
- wondering if you're doing enough
- managing *your* calendar *and* everyone else's expectations

This is called the mental load . . . and it's exhausting.

According to a 2025 working paper by Barigozzi and colleagues, individuals who take on a disproportionate share of mental labour – whether at home or at work – are significantly more likely to experience higher levels of emotional fatigue, burnout, depression and stress, and this can even carry over into worsening mental health at work.[2]

How to lighten the load (even when you can't drop the hats)

The goal isn't to do *less*.

It's to carry it *differently* – with more structure, more self-awareness and more support.

Here's how.

1. IDENTIFY WHAT'S YOURS TO HOLD

Sometimes we hold things out of habit or guilt, not necessity.

Take a moment and list out everything that's on your plate – personally, professionally, emotionally. Then ask:

- Does this actually *need* to be on me?
- Is there someone else who can support or share this?
- Am I carrying this because I feel I should, or because I genuinely want to?

You don't have to delegate everything. But you don't have to hold everything either.

One of my favourite books, *Drop the Ball* by Tiffany Dufu, completely changed how I view responsibility, especially as a woman who wears many hats.[3] Tiffany's philosophy is rooted in the idea that trying to do it all is not only unsustainable but unnecessary. By 'dropping the ball' – intentionally letting go of tasks that someone else could do – she redefined productivity not as perfection but as alignment with what truly matters. It was a liberating shift. Delegation isn't about giving up control; it's about creating space for what only *you* can do.

2. CREATE BOUNDARIES THAT DON'T FEEL LIKE WALLS

Boundaries aren't just about saying 'no'. They're about protecting the 'yes' that matters most.

Choose your non-negotiables: sleep, family dinner, workout time, focus hours.

Communicate them early – before burnout forces your hand.

Use tech tools to help (calendar blockers, email responders, scheduling apps).

Remember: your boundaries are not rude. They are *responsible*.

3. INTRODUCE THE 'LET THEM' THEORY (MEL ROBBINS)

Now, this one's a mindset shift I live by, especially as someone who has a tendency to overthink, and a best friend who proudly holds the presidency of the Overthinkers Society.

It's called the 'Let Them' theory, coined by Mel Robbins.

**If they don't agree with your comeback plan? Let them.
If they think you should have bounced back sooner?
Let them.
If they don't understand your boundaries, your
choices, your pace? Let them.**

Because while they're doubting, questioning, commenting, you are *moving*.

We hold so much emotional weight trying to micromanage how others perceive us. And it chips away at our resilience. 'Let them' is not about dismissing feedback or isolating yourself – it's about choosing peace over performance. Ownership over overthinking.

So, here's your reminder: let them think what they want. Let yourself do what you need.

4. TAKE BREAKS BEFORE YOU'RE BROKEN

Don't wait for burnout to justify rest.
    Schedule short, intentional pauses:

- a walk between meetings
- a quiet cup of tea without your phone
- a day off that isn't filled with errands
- five minutes of deep breathing after a challenging moment

Small resets create sustainability. They keep the engine running without forcing a breakdown.

5. REMEMBER THAT SEASONS CHANGE

There will be seasons when the load is heavier. A new baby. A product launch. A relocation. A personal crisis.

And there will be seasons when the pace slows and you get to recover.

Don't compare your current chapter to someone else's highlight reel. You're not falling behind – you're just in a different season.

Resilience isn't just bouncing back. It's carrying the weight with wisdom.

The Five Principles of Resilience

We've talked about resilience as a mindset, a science and a practice. But now let's bring it down to the ground level – the areas of life in which we live, work, love and lead.

Because setbacks don't only happen in business or in our careers. They happen in our relationships, our bodies, our homes, our dreams.

Resilience isn't compartmentalised. It's *whole-life armour*, and it flexes differently depending on where the hit lands.

Let's look at the Five Principles, where resilience matters most.

1. CAREER RESILIENCE

You didn't get the promotion.
Your manager changed, and now you feel invisible.
The company culture shifted. The restructure
happened. The budget disappeared.
Or maybe you've plateaued and can't see what's next.

Resilience here means:

- knowing your worth – even when someone else doesn't recognise it
- being willing to reskill or pivot
- activating your network when opportunities dry up
- not letting one rejection become a defining narrative

Reflection prompt: Where do I need to advocate for myself more confidently in my career?

2. ENTREPRENEURIAL RESILIENCE

Every founder, freelancer or side-hustler has *felt the sting.*

The product that flopped.
The client who ghosted.
The launch that didn't launch.
The imposter syndrome that shouts, 'You've peaked!'

Business resilience isn't just about persistence – it's about *adaptability*. The ability to try again *better*, not just harder. To audit what's working. To release what isn't. And to separate your self-worth from your sales figures.

Reflection prompt: Where is fear keeping me stuck in business – and what would a bolder version of me do next?

3. FAMILY AND RELATIONSHIP RESILIENCE

This principle is layered.

**It could be parenting with patience while running on fumes.
It could be navigating in-laws, separation or the loss of someone dear.
It could be maintaining connection with your partner during sleepless nights and growing pressures.
Or it could be *deciding who gets access to your energy at all*.**

Resilience in family and relationships means:

- communicating through tension, not avoiding it
- finding new rhythms after major changes
- setting boundaries with love, not guilt
- accepting that even your most important relationships will stretch you

Reflection prompt: Where is my energy being depleted in family life or in my relationships, and what would protect or restore it?

4. PERSONAL RESILIENCE (SELF)

Sometimes the biggest setback is . . . *you.*

**You didn't keep the promise you made to yourself.
You lost confidence. You feel behind. You're navigating identity changes that no one sees.**

Resilience here is the quiet rebuild.

- It's choosing not to give up on yourself.
- It's doing the inner work.
- It's waking up tomorrow and trying again.

Reflection prompt: What's one thing I need to forgive myself for, and how can I reconnect with my sense of purpose?

5. HEALTH RESILIENCE (MENTAL PLUS PHYSICAL)

**Your body's not responding the way it used to.
Your energy has shifted. Anxiety's creeping in.
Or you're navigating something more serious – an
injury, an illness, a diagnosis or perhaps simply sheer
exhaustion.**

Resilience in health means:

- listening to your body, not overriding it
- rebuilding with compassion, not punishment
- getting the support you need – whether that's a therapist, a trainer, a nutritionist or a walk in the park

Reflection prompt: What small act of care can I give my body or mind today without guilt?

Resilience isn't one-size-fits-all. But it is one-choice-at-a-time.

And across these Five Principles, it's the same truth repeating: you don't need to come back the same. You just need to come back *wiser*.

Reflection exercise: Resilience in real time

By now, you've probably realised that resilience isn't about some dramatic overnight comeback.

It's the quiet work. The invisible courage. The choosing-to-try-again, even when you could easily bow out.

You don't bounce back in a straight line. You bounce, pivot, pause, rebuild and evolve.

This chapter wasn't just about recovering from the big knockdowns; it's about building an inner structure so strong, so flexible, that when life tests you (and it will), *you know how to respond.*

Because true resilience isn't about pretending you're unaffected.

It's about moving with the waves and not losing your way in them.

Set aside some time – whether it's today or later this week – to reflect on where resilience is needed most in your life right now.

Pick a few of the following prompts that speak to you:

- Where in my life have I already demonstrated resilience, and what did it teach me?
- What setback has shaped me in ways I didn't expect?
- Which of the Five Principles feels the most out of balance right now, and why?
- What am I currently holding that isn't mine to carry?
- Who or what is fuelling my bounce-back right now, and who or what is draining it?
- If I applied the 'Let Them' mindset to one situation today, what would I release?

Your resilience action plan

Let's get practical. Choose at least one action for each principle of your life. These don't need to be huge shifts; they just need to move the needle forward.

CAREER

☐ Book a career conversation with your manager.
☐ Apply for a role that intimidates you – in a good way.
☐ Start documenting your wins weekly.

ENTREPRENEURSHIP

☐ Audit one area of your business that's draining you.
☐ Delegate a task that someone else could do 80 percent as well.
☐ Reach out to a peer for advice or a fresh perspective.

FAMILY AND RELATIONSHIPS

☐ Set one boundary to protect your energy.
☐ Schedule quality time that isn't centred on logistics.
☐ Ask for help – with no apology.

SELF

☐ Recommit to a daily routine that centres *you*.
☐ Forgive yourself for something that didn't go to plan.
☐ Speak to yourself the way you'd speak to a best friend.

HEALTH

☐ Book the appointment you've been putting off.
☐ Start or end your day with ten minutes of mindful movement.
☐ Choose one restorative habit to prioritise this week.

Setting the stage for success

You've got this!

Your ability to bounce back is not defined by what happened to you.

It's defined by how you show up for yourself in the aftermath.

And no matter what your bounce-back looks like – messy, slow, joyful, surprising, silent – know this: *you're still becoming*.

Every setback is an opportunity to prove to yourself just how powerful your comeback can be.

On to the next.

CHAPTER SEVEN
Creating a Supportive Network

You might be self-made, but you're not alone

When Bianca and I wrote our first book, *Self Made*, a few people took the title a little too literally.

They assumed we meant we'd done it all ourselves. No help. No guidance. No support. Just sheer grit and solo hustle.

Let me clear that up now: being self-made does not mean being self-sufficient to the point of isolation.

It means taking ownership of your journey.
It means building something from the ground up –
yes – but it also means having the vision to surround
yourself with people who elevate, challenge and
support you.

No successful entrepreneur or high-level career professional makes it entirely alone.

We all stand on the shoulders of others.

We're shaped by those who influence us – mentors, coaches, consultants, partners, parents, friends. The team behind the scenes is often the difference between a good idea that fizzles out and a powerful one that takes off.

Throughout my entrepreneurial journey, I've leaned on all the above.

Yes, I've paid for expertise – consultants, coaches, specialists – because when I want to go somewhere fast and smart, I don't waste time guessing.

But I've also leaned heavily on people like Bianca, close friends and trusted family members when I've needed perspective. When I've had to make a big decision, or when things haven't gone quite to plan.

Why? Because I trust that they've got my best interests at heart. And because I value collective thought. I might not always take their advice, but having it in the mix helps me make sharper decisions.

A supportive network is important in every area of life.

In fact, we probably would have moved to Dubai sooner if it weren't for one key thing: when it came time to give birth to our son, we knew that doing it in the UK – surrounded by Bianca's mum and her wider support system – was the right decision. That network mattered. Not just practically but emotionally. It made the journey smoother, safer, more grounded.

So no, 'self-made' doesn't mean you have to go it alone.

It means taking the lead *and* knowing when to let others walk with you.

And that's what this chapter is about – how to find, build and nurture the kind of network that doesn't just cheer for your success but also actively contributes to it.

The power of proximity

There's a quotation that's stuck with me ever since I heard it:

'Stop reading books and hire the author.'[1]

Belly Gene

Now, let's be clear – **that doesn't mean stop reading books.**

I still read, I still learn, I still invest in knowledge. But the *sentiment* behind that quote is powerful. Sometimes, the greatest impact doesn't come from *what* you read; it comes from *who* you get close to.

Reading someone's book gives you insight.

Hiring them? That gives you access, guidance, real-time answers and, often, a shortcut through the mistakes they've already made.

I've seen this principle play out time and time again in my own journey.

Some of the most pivotal decisions I've made in business have come from getting in the room with the people who had already done what I wanted to do. Whether that meant paying for their time, attending their events, or joining their programmes – it changed the game. The proximity gave me more than information. It gave me perspective, clarity and the confidence to execute.

This is also exactly how our Self Made Mentoring Programme was born.

After our debut book *Self Made* became a bestseller, we started getting messages from readers who called it a 'pocket mentoring experience'. They loved the book, but they wanted more. They wanted access. Hands-on support. Real-time, tailored advice. They wanted to be guided *through* the process, not just read *about* it.

That's the **power of proximity**.

To be close to someone who's already walked the path you're trying to walk means:

- you get to ask smarter questions
- you collapse your learning curve
- you stop guessing and start doing

We built a community of thriving entrepreneurs who went from concept to creation. Some started with nothing but an idea. Others had been stuck in second gear for years. But the moment they got into the right room – with the right mindset, structure and support – they accelerated. Some built six- and seven-figure businesses from scratch.

And not because we handed them success on a silver plate, but because we could show them *how* to get there – and walk alongside them while they did.

That's what proximity does. It closes the gap between where you are and where you want to be.

And if you're serious about manifested action – about turning vision into reality – you have to think about more than what you know. You have to think about who you know. Who's in your orbit? Who's done what you're trying to do? And how close are you willing to get?

Audit your circle

Let's be real: not everyone around you is rooting for your growth.

Some people are clapping because they think it's polite. Others are watching, quietly hoping you'll slow down – because your evolution makes them uncomfortable with their own stagnation. That's why, at some point in your journey, you have to audit your circle. The people closest to you either pull you forward or hold you in place.

This isn't about cutting people off or being ruthless. It's about being intentional.

Your goals are too important, and your time is too valuable to spend it being subtly undermined by people who can't see the future you're building.

Who's really in your inner circle?

Take a moment and ask yourself:

- Who do I speak to most often?
- Who do I turn to for advice, encouragement or a sounding board?
- Who do I allow to influence my decisions, even indirectly?
- Who gets the unfiltered version of me?

Now ask:

- Do these people elevate me or drain me?
- Are they comfortable with my ambition or quietly threatened by it?
- Do they challenge me to be better or encourage me to stay the same?
- When I share a win, do they cheer or go silent?

Sometimes, it's not the people yelling discouragement who hold you back. It's the ones offering just enough support to keep you doubting yourself. The subtle 'Are you sure that's a good idea?' The half-hearted 'That's amazing' with no follow-up.

The people who show up in your lows but go missing in your highs.

Redefining what support actually looks like

Support isn't just:

- being nice
- agreeing with everything you say
- showing up once in a while with a heart emoji

Support is:

- telling you the truth, even when it's uncomfortable
- celebrating your growth without comparison
- holding you accountable when you're playing small
- speaking your name in rooms you're not in
- reminding you who you are when you forget

You need people who see your vision, even when it's still blurry.

People who remind you what you said you wanted when you're tempted to settle.

Your circle is a mirror

Look around. Your current circle is a reflection of your current comfort zone.

If you're not growing, evolving or being challenged, it's time to shift your environment.

That doesn't always mean cutting people off. It might mean shifting the proximity.

Maybe they're still in your life but no longer on speed dial.
Maybe they stay for the memories, but they're not invited to shape your next move.

And that's okay.

You're allowed to grow in a direction that your past can't follow.

Build a circle that reflects your vision

If your vision is big, your circle needs to match it.

You don't build a multimillion-pound business, land your dream job or create generational impact by accident or in isolation.

You do it with intention. With structure. With the right people in your corner.

Bianca has always been strategic about this. One of her most powerful tools – one she's used with corporate leaders, founders and high-achieving professionals – is what she calls the Personal Board Framework.

Just like a successful company has a board of directors, she believes every person should have a board for their personal brand and personal success journey – whether that's in business, in a corporate career or in life overall.

This board isn't made up of formal appointments or stuffy titles. It's a mental structure. A framework. A guide to make sure you're not relying on one person to play every role, and that you're not missing the perspectives you need.

Here it is:

Bianca's Personal Board Framework

Challenger	Connector	Brand ambassador
They challenge your thoughts and goals, pushing you to look outside yourself to do more.	They're well networked, and while they may not have the knowledge or expertise, they can connect you with the right people.	They're influential and advocate for you, even when you're not in the room. They speak highly of your work and spread the word.

Life support	Expert	Loved one
When all else fails, this person props you up. They give you energy and emotional resilience, even in hard times.	The go-to person in your industry. They've done what you want to do and can align your vision with reality.	A person with whom you share a strong emotional bond – romantic or platonic. They provide the safety, love and intimacy that let you thrive.

Listener	Mentor	Client
This person gives you an ear whenever you need it; they are a safe sounding board for your ideas.	A constant in your life who has the knowledge and experience to provide you with the active next steps to enhance your career trajectory.	They are your target demographic. Maybe they were a client who has now become a friend and can provide you with the insight of a real customer – honest and helpful feedback that will help you to push your brand forward.

This framework helps you take your vision off the whiteboard and into the real world.

You might not have all nine roles filled right now, and that's okay. But it gives you clarity. It helps you see the gaps. It reminds you that taking consistent action isn't just about what you do; it's about who's helping you do it.

Manifestation without the right environment is like trying to grow a seed without soil.

Your board is your soil. Your climate. Your ecosystem for elevation.

As you grow, your board may evolve. People may shift roles. Some will step up. Others may fade out. That's part of the process.

The key is making sure that you're not walking alone when your vision is calling you to rise. Build your board like you'd build your legacy – with care, clarity and conviction.

Support systems vs safety nets

Not all support is created equal.

Some people in your life will lift you higher, stretch your potential and guide you through your next season. Others will wrap you in what feels like love, but, in reality, they're keeping you stuck. Not maliciously. Just . . . unknowingly. Often because they themselves are stuck, too.

It's essential to distinguish between a true support system and a safety net.

SUPPORT SYSTEMS HOLD YOU UP

Let's start with the real ones.

Supportive people in your life *don't flatter you so you feel useful.* They challenge you to expand. They'll say:

- 'How can I help you move this forward?'
- 'Have you thought about reaching higher?'
- 'You've done hard things before – this is just another one.'

They don't exist to rescue you. They exist to *remind you* who you are when you forget.

These are the mentors, coaches, colleagues, partners and friends who hold you accountable to the future version of you that you're working toward.

Their belief in you is practical. Tangible. Actionable.

SAFETY NETS HOLD YOU BACK

Then there's the *other* type of support – what I call comfort disguised as concern.

- They don't want you to get hurt.
- They don't want you to take risks.
- They'd rather you play small, stay local, keep things familiar.

And often, it's not because they don't love you. It's because *they can't imagine better for themselves.*

- They've never manifested beyond their postcode.
- They've never been surrounded by people chasing audacious goals.
- They've internalised a belief system that says, 'Be grateful for what you've got and don't get ahead of yourself.'
- Their fear becomes your caution tape.
- Their limitations start to sound like your logic.

If this sounds familiar, here's a cheeky but genuine suggestion: buy them their own copy. Highlight this chapter. Slide this book into their lives.

Not as a judgement, but as possibility.

Let them know there's another way to think, dream and support. Because, sometimes, they just haven't seen it modelled yet.

The trap of 'comfort friends'

Here's the truth: not everyone in your circle is meant to grow with you in every area.

Comfort friends are the people who love you as you *were* – not necessarily as who you're *becoming*. They're the friends from school who knew the 18-year-old version of you. The cousins who see you as the family joker, not the business owner. The old colleagues who still associate you with that entry-level role, not the boardroom you're gunning for now.

They love you. But their love lives in the past.

And if you're not careful, you'll shrink yourself just to stay lovable in their eyes. You'll flatten your dreams so they're easier to digest. You'll delay your action – not because *you* don't believe but because you're trying not to make *them* uncomfortable.

You need a diverse network

That's why it's not about ditching everyone – it's about diversifying your circle. You can have:

- friends who ground you
- friends who grow you
- friends who pour into your personal life
- friends who pour into your professional one
- friends who make you laugh
- friends who remind you to *level up*

Each serves a role. Not everyone has to be everything. But if no one in your circle challenges you to become more, it's time to step outside of it.

As Sheryl Sandberg writes in *Lean In*: 'Fortune does favour the bold, and you'll never know what you're capable of if you don't try.'[2]

You need people around you who push you to *try*. Who celebrate your boldness instead of cautioning you out of it. Who recognise your next level – even when you're still working through the current one.

Be a supportive force for others

It's easy to focus on what you need from others.

But one of the most powerful ways to build a supportive network – *and manifest the future you want* – is to first be a source of support yourself.

This isn't just about being a good friend or colleague. It's about showing up in the world with a Go-Giver mindset.

The Go-Giver philosophy, inspired by the brilliant book by Bob Burg and John David Mann,[3] is simple:

Focus on giving more value than you take.

Show up with generosity, intention and authenticity – and watch how the universe returns it to you.

I've seen this work in business, in life and in the most random interactions. When you show up to serve – not just to take – you create ripple effects you may not even realise are happening.

Networking is a reciprocal relationship

Let's be honest: most people hear the word 'networking' and think of awkward name tags, flat prosecco and the hope that someone in the room might be able to 'hook them up'.

But real networking isn't transactional; it's relational. It's not 'What can I get from you?' but 'How can we grow together?'

Networking is not about taking, it's about exchanging: energy, value, insight, support, referrals, wisdom, ideas.

When you start thinking about every connection as a two-way street, something shifts. You stop hoarding your knowledge. You become a door-opener. A connector. A true asset in someone else's journey.

And guess what? That energy circles back to you.

Give – and the universe gives back

Manifestation isn't just about writing goals in a journal and waiting for the magic to happen.

It's about action. Alignment. And, yes, *reciprocity*.

When you give time, energy, kindness, knowledge, encouragement, you create space to receive. The universe responds to momentum. And the momentum starts with you.

You want support? Support someone else.
You want a mentor? Be a mentor.
You want to be remembered? Start by adding value.

If you're more spiritually minded, think of it this way: the energy you put out becomes the energy you attract.

And for those of us grounded in faith, the principle is the same. The Bible, for example, tells us in Luke 6:38: 'Give, and it will be given to you. A good measure, pressed down, shaken together and running over, will be poured into your lap.'[4]

Whatever language you use – universal law, karma, sowing and reaping – the lesson is clear:

When you show up to serve, you're always planting seeds for your own future harvest.

Who you are when no one's watching matters

Some of the most valuable relationships in my life have come not from pitching myself but from *helping someone else get ahead*:

- a word of encouragement
- a connection made quietly
- a 'you need to meet this person' moment
- a resource shared without expecting anything in return

These are the moments people remember.

These are the reasons people invite you into rooms, into partnerships, into opportunities you couldn't have imagined.

Because they don't just see your talent – they see your character.

So, as you build your board, expand your circle and seek your next level . . . Ask yourself not just 'Who do I need?' but 'Who can I be?'

Because when you give from a place of wholeness – not desperation – you become the magnet for everything you've been trying to manifest.

Leveraging your network to build wealth

Let's be clear: being generous with your time, energy and knowledge doesn't mean you can't also build wealth through your network.

We've already said networking is not just transactional – it's relational. But relationships can still create real financial value. In fact, they *should*.

Over the course of my career, I've earned over six figures *just through connections*. Not by cold pitching. Not by slick sales tricks. But by introducing the right people to each other – at the right time – and being rewarded with commission or a referral fee.

You'd be surprised how many people are happy to pay when you solve a problem for them that they didn't know how to fix on their own.

That's what real value looks like. It's not just about your direct product or service. It's about your access. Your insight. Your ability to connect dots and create win–win scenarios.

We apply this philosophy in every one of our businesses. Whether it's our mentoring programmes, consultancy or speaking engagements, if someone refers us a client, we offer a referral fee as standard. Why? Because referral marketing is one of the strongest forms of marketing there is.

If someone has a great experience with you, why wouldn't you *incentivise* them to share it? You're not buying loyalty. You're rewarding impact.

Bianca's story: When relationships lead to the boardroom

Bianca is one of the most powerful examples I've seen of how a well-nurtured personal brand and authentic relationship-building can open unimaginable doors.

Throughout the 14 years she's been running her business, her network has played a massive role in its growth. Clients don't just book her once; they refer her across departments, to other companies, and even internationally.

But the moment that still blows me away happened during the pandemic.

We were in Dubai, navigating life as digital nomads. Bianca had been journaling her experience in a series of thoughtful, honest articles for *Forbes*. One article casually mentioned her stay at the FIVE

Palm Jumeirah Hotel – not as an advert, but as part of her lived experience.

That week, she got a call from a new contact in Dubai. The founder and CEO of FIVE wanted to meet her. That one meeting turned into a friendship. And that friendship turned into something no one could've predicted ...

She was invited to join the board of this multibillion-dollar global hospitality brand. No formal pitch. No application. Just reputation. Authenticity. Value. And the kind of network magnetism that only happens when you *show up* fully and consistently.

All of it – manifested through action.

Because that's what happens when your personal brand is strong, your network is nurtured, and your values align with the opportunities around you.

And the best part? She hadn't even considered this as part of her vision. It came because she'd built a reputation that did the talking for her.

This is what we mean when we say manifested action. It's not just about what you're working on; it's about who you're becoming ... and how your network reflects that back to you in ways you could never have predicted.

The Five Principles of Support

Support doesn't always look the same, and it shouldn't.

In fact, depending on where you are in your life, the type of support you need in each area can differ drastically. The people who help you navigate career growth might not be the same ones who support your mental health, or help you parent, or hold you accountable to your goals.

That's why it's important to assess your circle through the lens of the Five Principles of Manifested Action.

If your environment is your ecosystem, then your support system is the climate that makes everything grow.

Let's break this down.

1. CAREER SUPPORT

You're not meant to climb the ladder alone or reinvent it from scratch. Career support might look like:

- a mentor or sponsor within your organisation who advocates for your growth
- a colleague who keeps you accountable to your development goals
- a former manager who still coaches you informally
- someone who introduces you to new opportunities, industries or projects

If you're changing direction, levelling up or simply trying to stay inspired in a long-term role, career support is your compass.

Ask yourself: Who knows the version of my career I'm trying to build, and how often do I talk to them?

2. ENTREPRENEURSHIP SUPPORT

Entrepreneurship can be isolating – unless you build a table of allies. Here, support might look like:

- a business mentor who's been where you're trying to go
- a mastermind group that challenges and refines your ideas
- a team member who believes in your mission and pushes you towards better leadership
- a community of peers who celebrate your wins and normalise your challenges

Ask yourself: Do I have people around me who understand what it takes to build and scale something, and do they see the gaps I might be missing?

3. FAMILY SUPPORT

Whether you're single, partnered, a parent or caring for others, family life can be full-on. And support here can be as emotional as it is logistical.

Support might look like:

- a partner who shares domestic and emotional labour
- a parent or sibling who shows up during your busy seasons
- a friend who checks in on your wellbeing, not just your productivity
- extended family or chosen family who contribute to your child's growth and your peace of mind

This principle matters *deeply*, especially for those navigating high-achievement lifestyles.

Ask yourself: Do I feel seen, supported and emotionally safe in my closest relationships?

4. SELF SUPPORT

This is the one most people forget.

Support for yourself might look like:

- a coach or therapist who helps you grow through what you go through
- a spiritual guide or practice that keeps you anchored
- a close friend who reminds you of your worth
- *you*, showing up for yourself with rest, honesty and care

Ask yourself: Am I prioritising my own evolution, or am I pouring from an empty cup?

5. HEALTH SUPPORT (MENTAL AND PHYSICAL)

Burnout doesn't ask if you're busy. It shows up anyway. So does stress. Anxiety. Injury. Illness. Preventative care is support, too.

Support might look like:

- a great GP or specialist you trust
- a physiotherapist who helps you stay consistent and strong
- a wellness buddy who walks with you or trains with you
- a support group or community that shares your health journey

Ask yourself: Who is helping me protect my energy, body and clarity – without judgement?

You don't need to have every principle perfect. But you do need awareness.

Because support isn't a luxury. It's part of the strategy.

You're allowed to ask for help.

You're allowed to outgrow unhelpful patterns.

And you're allowed to build the kind of ecosystem that doesn't just help you survive, but helps you *thrive*.

Reflection exercise: Audit – align – activate

Your network is either nurturing your growth or unknowingly stifling it.

It's not always about cutting people off. It's about aligning your environment with your goals. About making intentional choices about who gets access to your time, your energy, and your ideas.

Because, when your circle reflects the version of yourself you're becoming, and not just the version you've been, everything accelerates.

This chapter wasn't just about building a feel-good community. It was about surrounding yourself with the kind of people who activate action, hold you accountable, and support the weight of the vision you're carrying.

And yes, it's about *being* that person for others, too.

Take some time to sit with the following questions. They're not just for now; they're for whenever your circle, your goals or your growth starts to shift.

1 **Who in my life challenges me to rise?**

_____

_____

_____

2 **Who in my life subtly encourages me to shrink?**

_____

_____

_____

3 **Which of the Five Principles (career, entrepreneurship, family and relationships, self, health) needs more support, and where can I start?**

_____

_____

_____

4 **What role do I currently play in other people's networks? Am I giving what I hope to receive?**

_____

_____

5 **Who am I inspired to reconnect with, invest in or meet in the next 90 days?**

_____

_____

_____

Action plan: Building your network with purpose

- **Complete your personal board audit.** Refer back to Bianca's Personal Board Framework. Who do you already have in place? Who's missing? Who could shift roles?
- **Book one conversation this month.** Reach out to a mentor, potential partner or peer who inspires you. Not to pitch – just to connect with intention.
- **Join one room that matches your next level.** This could be a mastermind, a professional group, a live event or a digital community. Proximity changes everything.
- **Be generous first.** Introduce two people in your network who could benefit from knowing each other. Add value with no agenda.
- **Decide how you want to show up.** Are you the Challenger? The Connector? The Sponsor? Choose a role you want to play in someone else's growth, and commit to it.

Setting the stage for success

Your future doesn't just depend on your effort. It depends on your ecosystem.

So build it with precision. Nourish it with intention. And let it carry you through seasons where momentum alone isn't enough.

Because when you surround yourself with people who make action inevitable, manifestation becomes inevitable, too.

CHAPTER EIGHT
Balancing Work and Life

Redefining what balance really means

When people hear the word 'balance', the image that often springs to mind is that of a traditional scale – each side weighed perfectly, suspended in a moment of harmonious equilibrium. It's a nice idea in theory. But in practice? That kind of balance is largely a myth.

In real life, the scales are in constant motion. Some days they tip towards your work; other days they tip towards your family and relationships, your health, your sanity – or even chaos. Often, just when you feel you've finally mastered this intricate juggling act, something shifts. A child gets sick, a project deadline is brought forward, or you realise you haven't had a decent night's sleep in over a week. The scale tips again, and you're back to recalibrating.

I (Bianca) have always been someone who sits firmly on the side of optimism. I'm a believer in the power of a positive mental attitude and the idea that we can create lives of fulfilment, success and joy if we're intentional enough. I truly believe you can have it all – but *can you have it all at the same time?* I think you can. Just not in equal measure. Not every day. Not every week. Not every season.

I've manifested a life I love. A life that allows me to express my full self – founder, author, entrepreneur, speaker, consultant, wife, daughter, friend and, more recently, mother. But each new role I've taken on hasn't replaced the previous ones. It's not about choosing one over the other. Instead, each has added new strings to the instrument I'm learning to play. The music is still mine – it's just more layered now.

Since becoming a mother, I've made an intentional choice to phase my return to work. In practice, this looks like working three days a week on the business, dedicating three days fully to our son and our family, and keeping one day completely for myself – to reset, to rest, to see friends or to simply *be*. Is it always a perfect split? Of course not. Do I appreciate the weeks when it flows that way? Immensely. Because in those moments, I feel like I'm getting the best of both worlds.

But balance, as I've come to understand it, isn't about symmetry. It's about rhythm. It's about feeling present where I am, when I'm there. It's about recognising the season I'm in and making choices that align with my values – not a fantasy idea of what my life 'should' look like.

There's also a narrative – particularly aimed at mothers – that says: if you enjoy your work, if you pursue ambition or if you carve out time for yourself, you must somehow be neglecting your child. That guilt creeps in like a thief, robbing you of the joy that comes from loving *all* the roles you play.

But here's my truth: choosing to honour my work does not diminish my love for my child. In fact, it strengthens it. When I'm doing work that lights me up, when I'm feeling fulfilled, when I'm growing professionally and personally, I show up as a more grounded, more energised, more loving parent. My son gets a version of me that is full, not depleted. And as he grows, I want him to witness what it looks like to see a woman not only nurture others but nurture herself. To love deeply and to lead boldly.

And it's not just about mothers. Over the years I've worked with clients – some of them incredibly high-net-worth individuals – who technically don't need to work another day in their lives. They've secured their legacies. But they still show up with passion, with hunger, and with a desire to *create*. Why? Because the work brings them joy. It gives them purpose. One of my clients once said to me, 'I don't need the money, Bianca. But what else would I do? I want my children to see what's possible. I want them to see what it looks like to build something meaningful.'

That mindset has always stuck with me. Because what we model – whether in motherhood, marriage, mentorship or management – sets the tone for how others define fulfilment for themselves.

So, this chapter isn't about chasing an unrealistic picture of perfect balance. It's about creating a version of life that feels aligned. It's about defining success on your terms. Whether your season calls for stillness or sprinting, raising children or raising capital, this chapter is your permission slip to build a life that reflects what you value – not what anyone else expects of you.

Let's redefine what balance really means.

Defining your own version of balance

One of the biggest misconceptions about balance is that it's some-thing you arrive at. As if one day, with enough clever diary manage-ment and the right meditation app, your life will suddenly slide into perfect alignment. You'll glide through your days, never dropping a ball, never forgetting a birthday, always feeling calm, productive, con-nected and fulfilled.

In reality, balance is not a destination – it's a fluid, ever-shifting concept. And, more importantly, it's entirely personal.

What feels balanced for one person may feel suffocating or chaotic for another. Your version of balance must reflect your values, your respon-sibilities, your aspirations and – crucially – the season of life you're in.

I've met women who run billion-pound companies and still make the school run a non-negotiable. I've met stay-at-home fathers who are building their second business in the hours between nap time and nursery pick-up. Balance looks like *whatever works for you* – not what social media, outdated societal norms, or even well-meaning friends think it should look like.

And it's important to remember that balance will evolve as you do.

When Beyoncé said 'no'

Take Beyoncé, for example. In a 2020 *Vogue* interview, she spoke openly about restructuring her life after years of touring, creating and pushing herself to the limit. She shared that, after becoming a mother, her definition of success shifted. It wasn't just about the music or the accolades – it became about joy, presence, and protecting her mental and physical health. That included saying 'no' more often, limiting media exposure and prioritising time with her family.

This wasn't about slowing down out of necessity; it was about choosing a new rhythm that aligned with who she had become.

It was about *balance*, Beyoncé style.

Barack Obama's 'evening rule'

Barack Obama, during his presidency – arguably one of the most demanding jobs on earth – shared a very simple but powerful practice: he made it a rule to sit down and eat dinner with his daughters every evening, no matter what. That boundary wasn't just about fatherhood. It was a deliberate decision to stay grounded, to remain connected to his personal values while navigating extraordinary responsibility.

That one choice was a declaration: *my version of balance includes family first, even in the most pressured environments.*

What balance doesn't have to be

Let me be clear: defining your own version of balance doesn't mean you've got it all figured out. It doesn't mean your inbox is always at zero or your children never throw tantrums at inconvenient times (if only!). It simply means that you're clear about your priorities and that you've built a structure around them that *mostly* works – and when it doesn't, you're kind enough to yourself to make adjustments without guilt.

It also doesn't mean you have to adhere to anyone else's version of fulfilment.

You don't need to 'do it all' to be worthy.

You don't need to monetise every hobby.

And you absolutely don't need to apologise for wanting either more ambition or more peace in your life.

You get to decide what your version of success looks like – and design your life accordingly.

A personal invitation to reflect

If this chapter does anything, I hope it encourages you to pause and ask:

- What do I really want my days to feel like?
- What rhythms make me feel connected, energised and purposeful?
- Am I living according to someone else's idea of balance, or my own?
- What am I no longer available for?

Because balance isn't about doing everything.

It's about doing the *right* things, at the *right* time, for *your* version of success.

And that version may not be popular. It may not be palatable to everyone. But it's yours – and that's what makes it powerful.

Time is not the enemy – lack of clarity is

There's a viral quote that resurfaces every few months on social media, often dropped like a truth bomb: 'You have the same 24 hours as Beyoncé.'

It's usually delivered with motivational flair, often backed by some slow-mo gym footage or a power playlist.

But a few years ago, a well-known influencer and entrepreneur, Molly-Mae Hague, reignited the debate when she used a version of this line in an interview. She said something along the lines of, 'We all have the same 24 hours in a day,' and the internet exploded.

People were furious. And, I'll be honest, I could kind of understand the backlash. Because while the statement is technically true, it completely lacks context.

Of course we all have 24 hours in a day. That's basic physics.

But we *don't* all have the *same* 24 hours.

Some people wake up to nannies, personal chefs and virtual assistants. Others wake up to school runs, night shifts or caring for ageing parents.

Molly-Mae, by her own admission, had built a level of financial success that allowed her to *buy help*. Help with her home, her business and her baby. And that help? That's what gives her time. That's what gives her capacity. That's what allows her to live her 'same 24 hours' very differently from someone juggling life solo.

What I found fascinating was not just the outrage, but where that outrage was directed.

Why were people so angry at *her* for using her time differently? Why not direct that energy inward? Or, better yet, ask more interesting questions:

- What have I done with *my* 24 hours?
- How do I want to use them differently?
- And what am I willing to change in order to create a life that feels less frantic and more fulfilling?

Because here's the real point: the problem isn't time.

The problem is *clarity*.

If you're unclear on what matters to you, how can you possibly manage your time in a way that reflects your values?

When time feels like the villain

We've all had those days when we feel like time is out to get us. The to-do list is endless, the emails keep coming, the child won't nap, and just when you think you've carved out a moment for yourself, someone utters the dreaded phrase: 'Have you got a quick sec?'

The day slips by, the guilt creeps in, and suddenly it's 10 p.m. and you're asking: 'What did I even do today?'

On the flip side, we've also had moments when time felt generous. A quiet morning before the house wakes up. A holiday where the days feel long and the sunsets feel earned.

But maybe time isn't the issue. Maybe it's our relationship to it.

Clarity over calendar

Time is fixed, but clarity is flexible. And clarity is what turns your time into *intention*.

If you're not clear on your priorities, your values or the life you're trying to build, it doesn't matter how colour-coded your Google Calendar is. You'll still feel like you're running behind.

The question isn't just: 'How do I manage my time better?' It's: 'What matters most to me right now, and how do I protect time for it?'

A quick self-audit: Are you making time or losing it?

Here's a simple framework to help you start reframing your time through the lens of clarity:

- What do I want more of in my week (e.g. focus, connection, creativity, rest)?
- What drains me that I keep doing out of habit or obligation?
- What can I delegate, decline or defer without guilt?
- When during the day am I at my best, and am I protecting that time?
- Am I spending more time reacting . . . or creating?

You don't need a fancy productivity system to feel more in control of your time. You just need a better understanding of *why* you're doing what you're doing, and what you're willing to sacrifice for it.

Making time your friend

Balance isn't about squeezing more into the same 24 hours. It's about redefining what fills those hours in the first place.

It's about *choosing* how you spend your time based on what truly matters to you – not what's trending, expected or performative.

And yes, we can acknowledge the realities of privilege, access and circumstance while also empowering ourselves to move with intention.

The goal isn't perfection. It's clarity.

Because when you're clear, your time becomes a tool – not a trap.

The role of delegation and support

Let's have an honest conversation about something that gets wildly overlooked in discussions about work-life balance: *delegation.*

There's a common misconception that delegation is something reserved for executives, CEOs or people with large teams at their disposal. But, in reality, **delegation is a mindset shift** – and it's one that every person, whether you're a stay-at-home parent, a solopreneur or a corporate professional, can benefit from adopting.

So many of us are overwhelmed, burnt out and stretched thin, not because we're doing too much, but because we're doing too much *of the wrong things.* Things that someone else could do, would happily do and might even do better – *if* we could just let go of the need to do it all ourselves.

But for some reason, the idea of asking for help – especially with household or admin tasks – still challenges people. I've spent years telling friends, clients, even family members to consider outsourcing where they can. To pay for peace. To protect their time. To stop wearing exhaustion like a badge of honour. And I've been met with *outrage.*

It's as if hiring a cleaner or using a PA means you think you're too good to mop your own floors or respond to your own emails.

But that's not the point.

It starts with letting go of the belief that you have to do it all.

Or, worse, that doing it all makes you somehow morally superior.

The 'broke-ass decision' mindset shift

In her brilliant book *We Should All be Millionaires*, Rachel Rodgers introduces the concept of the 'broke-ass decision'.[1]

It's not about being poor or rich. It's about mindset. She describes broke-ass decisions as the small, day-to-day choices we make that keep us stuck – like spending our time on tasks that don't generate income, don't contribute to our peace of mind, don't move us closer to our goals and absolutely *do not* reflect our worth.

These decisions aren't always about money. Sometimes they're about self-worth. Sometimes they're about old narratives that tell us we're not 'deserving' of help. But they always come at a cost. A cost to our time. A cost to our energy. A cost to our potential.

She gives examples like:

- spending three hours cleaning your bathroom instead of spending one hour resting and two hours working on your side hustle
- spending hours manually doing admin you could automate
- refusing to invest in support, even though you spend every night exhausted and behind

And listen: I've been preaching this gospel long before I had a name for it. I wish I'd had Rachel's language at the time, because it perfectly captures what I've been trying to get people to understand.

Let's get a cleaner

When Byron and I bought our first home together, I knew we needed to have *the talk*.

Not the financial one – we'd covered that.

Not the decor one – that was already under way.

No, this was the domestic one.

I looked at him and said, 'So, do you plan to clean?'

He looked unsure. Not because he didn't want a clean home – we both love a clean home – but because, realistically, neither of us had the time or inclination to deep-clean after a full day's work.

So I made a suggestion that changed our lives: 'Let's get a cleaner.'

He agreed. And we never looked back.

That £8–12 per hour (this was over 15 years ago) wasn't just paying for sparkling floors. It was an investment in *peace*. It meant fewer arguments, more time to spend together, and more energy we could redirect into growing our businesses and our relationship.

We wanted a soft life – and we were willing to pay for it in smart ways. That one decision bought us freedom, clarity and more time to do the things that truly mattered.

Delegation isn't always financial

Now let me be clear: delegation doesn't always mean hiring a team. Sometimes it's about clever systems. Sometimes it's about asking your partner, your kids or your colleagues to step up. Sometimes it's about simply *letting go* of the idea that you have to do it all to be worthy.

Here are a few ways to start thinking differently about delegation:

- **Domestic support** If you're spending your weekends deep-cleaning instead of resetting, resting or working on your goals, ask yourself: 'Could someone else do this?' That might mean hiring a cleaner, or it might mean starting a rota with your partner or housemates. Either way, your time has value.
- **Food and errands** Automate your grocery shop. Batch-cook on Sundays. Use a meal kit or delivery app if that gives you back an hour of sanity. These aren't luxuries – they're life-design choices.
- **Business or work tasks** Whether you're a solopreneur or managing a team, don't hold on to every task out of fear or ego. What could be handed off? Automated? Scheduled in advance? Delegation is the difference between scaling and stalling.
- **Mental-load sharing** If you're managing the social calendar, the family logistics and the reminders for everyone else, you are carrying the mental load. And it's time to redistribute that. Shared calendars, to-do lists, open communication: all small ways to free your brain for *bigger things*.
- **Skill-based outsourcing** Byron often says, 'Buy the shortcut.' If someone knows more, has done it faster or can execute better than you, hire them. Time is the one thing you can't earn back, so invest in support that accelerates your success.

The power of buying back time

Delegation is about *creating capacity*. Capacity for rest. Capacity for creativity. Capacity for income.

You cannot manifest your dream life if every hour is spent doing the things that drain you.
You cannot move toward abundance if your time is consumed by survival.

And to be clear – this isn't about privilege. This is about *choice*. About resourcefulness. About valuing your time, and using what you *do* have to buy back what you don't.

Maybe for you, the next step isn't hiring a cleaner or a virtual assistant.
Maybe it's automating your invoices.
Maybe it's batch-cooking once a week.
Maybe it's asking your partner to take over bedtime a few nights a week.
Maybe it's finally saying no to that commitment you dread every month.

The question isn't just: 'What can I delegate?' It's: 'What would my life feel like if I stopped doing things that don't serve me?'
Instead of asking, 'Can I afford this?' ask:

- 'What would it cost me to keep doing it all?'
- 'What would I do with that time if I had it back?'
- 'What am I trying to prove by doing this alone?'

The truth is, you're not meant to do it all. You're meant to do what only *you* can do, and build a life where you are supported, not stretched.

Why this matters for manifested action

Manifestation is about clarity.
Action is about intentionality.

And delegation is the bridge between wanting time and actually creating it.

If you want to manifest a life that feels calm, productive and aligned, you must be willing to release control over the tasks that don't serve you.

Your time is your currency. Don't spend it on things that deplete you when you could be investing it in what brings you closer to your vision.

Building sustainable self-care

Let's set the record straight: self-care is not a luxury. It's not all scented candles, spa days or yoga retreats, though I enjoy all three when I can. True self-care is a foundational part of being able to show up for your life with clarity, creativity and consistency.

But somewhere along the way, the conversation around self-care became commercialised. It started to feel like something you *buy* rather than something you *build*. The result? So many high-performing, goal-orientated people – especially women – see self-care as something they'll 'get to later'. After the launch. After the kids are in bed. After the inbox is cleared. After the world stops demanding so much from them.

But here's the truth I've come to learn: if your self-care isn't sustainable, your success won't be either.

You cannot pour from an empty cup. You cannot serve, build or lead if you're constantly running on fumes.

You can't manifest your dream life if you're too exhausted to visualise it, let alone pursue it.

Redefining self-care

Self-care isn't about escape – it's about energy management.

It's about recovery.

It's about creating rituals and routines that nourish you from the inside out so that you can stay in the game long enough to see your vision become reality.

Here's what sustainable self-care can look like in real life:

- **Boundaries that honour your energy** Saying no to the meeting that could be an email. Saying no to the event that drains you. Saying no to people who only come around to take, not to give. Saying no to that opportunity that is unpaid.
- **Daily practices that reset your nervous system** This could be a morning walk, journaling, five minutes of deep breathing, or even just stepping away from your desk for lunch *without your phone*. It doesn't have to be dramatic – it just has to be deliberate.
- **Physical movement you actually enjoy** Not for aesthetics, but for release. For strength. For vitality. That might be dance, weightlifting, Pilates, yoga, swimming, or even wrestling with your toddler on the floor (which, trust me, counts as cardio).
- **Sleep that is protected, not postponed** Your brain needs rest. Your body needs restoration. The world can wait for your reply.
- **Joy for joy's sake** Do things that make you laugh, that bring you lightness, that remind you who you are outside of your responsibilities. Sometimes the most radical form of self-care is to simply do something fun *with no outcome attached*.

When it all feels like too much

I know what it feels like to be in a season where the to-do list is so long that even your 'rest' feels scheduled.

When I had my son, the hours bled into each other. My sleep came in 90-minute shifts. The days were loud, and the nights were quiet but never restful. There were moments I wasn't sure where the old me had gone.

But I learned to build new rituals. Little things. Small signals to my mind and body that I still mattered, too:

- my morning tea in silence
- a stretch in the lounge while Ethan napped
- a call with a friend where we didn't talk about work or babies, just music, and gossip, and life

You don't need a spa day. You need *space*. (But book the spa day anyway. I did. It was great!)

How to build a personal self-care framework

Let's stop waiting for time to appear and start creating it. Here's a guide to start embedding self-care into your everyday life:

- **Audit your week.** Look at how you actually spend your time. Where are your energy leaks? Where do you feel the most drained?
- **Identify one habit to release.** What are you doing out of guilt, obligation or autopilot that you can let go of – even just for now?
- **Choose one habit to protect.** Is there something that refuels you that you're constantly pushing aside? Choose to keep it, even in small doses.
- **Schedule your joy.** Treat your joy like a non-negotiable calendar event. Put it in your diary like you would a meeting with your boss or client.
- **Ask for help before you hit the wall.** Don't wait until you're depleted. If you need rest, support or space – say it. Delegate. Reschedule. Reorganise. Honour the signal.

You are not a machine. You are not a martyr.

You are a human being with a mind, body and soul that deserve to be nurtured – not just on weekends or holidays, but *every day*, in small and meaningful ways.

Because the version of you that is well-rested, well-nourished and well-loved? That's the version of you that will manifest the life you dream about, and that will actually enjoy it when it arrives.

Primed for greatness: The power of routine

Over the years, I've had the pleasure of learning from some of the best in the business when it comes to performance, discipline and intentional living. One of those people is Lewis Paris, a trainer and longevity strategist whose work with elite athletes, career professionals and leaders is rooted in one central idea: how you live your days is how you live your life.

I often refer to Lewis as a 'longevity strategist', because he doesn't just coach for performance – he coaches for sustainability. For rhythm. For real-world routines that help people live longer, stronger and more aligned lives. And while not every schedule works for every lifestyle, there is a growing body of research that suggests **routine is a key predictor of success**.

A study published in *Frontiers in Psychology* found that people with structured daily routines report higher levels of emotional stability and lower levels of stress and anxiety. Why? Because routine reduces cognitive load. It frees your brain to focus on what matters most, instead of spending energy constantly deciding what's next.[2]

Lewis has created a daily rhythm that helps his clients increase their productivity, performance and peace – not by doing more, but by doing what matters.

Take inspiration from his system below and use the accompanying checklist to reflect, adapt and create a rhythm that serves your season.

A daily rhythm for performance and peace

'I created this routine not to impress anyone, but to rescue myself from burnout. I was constantly chasing peak performance but ignoring recovery. Eventually, I realised: routine doesn't restrict you – *it frees you*. When your day starts with intention, everything else follows with purpose.'

EVENING ROUTINE (WIND DOWN)

Begin winding down from 9 p.m.:

- Drink a mug of herbal tea.
- Do some journaling or note-taking: today's wins and losses.
- Prepare bag and clothes for the next day.
- Do 5–10 minutes of mobility or stretching.
- Take a shower or bath.

In bed by 9.45–10 p.m.:

- Read a book for 20–30 minutes.
- Switch off the lights by 10.30 p.m.
- Trouble sleeping? Try white noise or meditation music.

MORNING ROUTINE (WAKE READY)

Wake between 5 a.m. and 5.30 a.m.:

- Make the bed.
- Do some physical activity (mobility drills, jog or workout – 15–30 minutes).
- Brush teeth and shower.
- Get dressed and prepare for the day.
- Delay coffee intake until 60–90 minutes after waking.
- Journal intentions, gratitudes and key objectives.
- Prepare or eat a nourishing breakfast.
- Begin your deep work.

DAILY NON-NEGOTIABLES

- Take a morning cold shower.
- Journal (morning and afternoon).
- Read a chapter before bed.

WEEKLY NON-NEGOTIABLES

- Devote three sessions of 30 minutes to call family/friends.
- Try something new or explore locally once a week.

Create your own rhythm: Checklist template

Adapt the prompts below to fit your lifestyle.

EVENING WIND-DOWN (FROM 9 p.m.)

_____

_____

_____

_____

_____

LIGHTS-OUT TIME

_____

_____

_____

_____

MORNING ROUTINE (WAKE-UP TIME)

_____

_____

_____

_____

PREPARATION FOR THE DAY

_____

_____

_____

_____

_____

DAILY NON-NEGOTIABLES

_____

_____

_____

_____

_____

WEEKLY NON-NEGOTIABLES

_____

_____

_____

_____

_____

Routine breeds productivity.

Routine isn't rigid – it's freedom in disguise. The less time you spend deciding what's next, the more time you have to move with purpose. As Lewis says, 'You don't need to be perfect. Just 1 percent better each day compounds to massive results.'

So whether your rhythm includes a 5 a.m. workout or five minutes of silence before the day begins, know this: consistency creates clarity. Clarity creates action. And action? As Lewis would say: 'That's how you stay dangerous.'

Please don't forget to share your new routine with Lewis on Instagram @lewisparisfitness (tag us, too!).

Pressures of modern living

Modern life is relentless.

It's not just the to-do list that overwhelms us – it's the *thinking* about the to-do list. It's not just the work calls, the business strategies or the client deliverables – it's the mental gymnastics of keeping everything afloat that silently chips away at our energy.

This is what we call the mental load.

It's the weight of remembering the milk, scheduling the dentist, prepping for the presentation, replying to the email, following up with the nursery, planning dinner, remembering birthdays, keeping up with your brand on LinkedIn, being an engaged partner, and somehow also finding time to meditate.

It's invisible, it's exhausting, and – more often than not – it falls disproportionately on women.

But let's be clear: this isn't just a woman's issue. Yes, women have historically carried more of this load, but anyone living a multifaceted life – managing a home, building a career, raising children, supporting ageing parents or navigating relationships – knows exactly what this kind of pressure feels like.

My mental-load story: All the hats, all at once

When I became a mum, I didn't stop being an entrepreneur. I didn't stop being a speaker, a strategist, a mentor, a founder, a wife, a daughter, a friend. The world didn't stop turning, and neither did the calendar.

I was, as they say, *in it*.

And while I have an incredibly supportive husband in Byron, who took on night shifts, managed the businesses, and made sure I was supported in every way possible, the mental load still sat heavily with me at times. Because, even with help, I was still carrying the planning, the anticipating, the emotional processing of what our lives needed next.

It wasn't just about doing the work – it was about holding the vision, every day.

Let's talk about overthinking

At one point, I joked with a friend – the 'president of the Overthinkers Society' – that sometimes the heaviest thing I carry is my own brain. The looping thoughts, the second-guessing, the *what ifs*. It's not just worrying about what needs to get done – it's worrying about whether we're doing enough, being enough, becoming enough.

As mentioned in Chapter 6, this is why I love Mel Robbins's 'Let Them' theory. She says:

- If people don't understand your boundaries – let them.
- If people think you've changed – let them.
- If people underestimate you – let them.

Because too often, our mental load is made heavier by trying to control how others perceive us. By worrying about reactions we can't manage or opinions that don't pay our bills.

Sometimes the most liberating thing you can do is *drop the rope*.

Let them. Let go. Breathe.

Stress is more than just tiredness

We throw around the word 'stress' casually, but it's a serious thing. Chronic stress impacts our mood, sleep, digestion, focus, immunity and long-term health. It's a silent saboteur.

For some, it shows up as anxiety. For others, as brain fog. For many, as burnout.

And burnout isn't just about being tired – it's emotional depletion, mental exhaustion and the loss of joy in things that once inspired you.

As mentioned in Chapter 5, if high-profile, high-achieving individuals like Whitney Wolfe Herd and Prince Harry can take a very visible step back for their mental health, *why do we think we can't?*

Managing the load

So how do we manage the mental load while continuing to take action on our dreams? Here are a few steps to lighten the weight while maintaining the juggle:

1 **Identify what's yours to hold.** Not everything is your responsibility. Tiffany Dufu's *Drop the Ball* reframed this for me (see Chapter 6). She writes about how women in particular feel obligated to carry it all – but often, they don't *need* to. Delegation isn't failure. It's strategy.

2 **Get clear on what matters this week – not forever.** Goals are long-term, but pressure is daily. Focus on what actually needs your energy today, not every dream all at once.

3 **Speak your needs out loud.** Don't wait for burnout to ask for help. Don't assume people can see how much you're holding. Be clear, be kind and be specific.

4 **Create mental 'off' moments.** Whether it's walking in silence, switching off your notifications, or simply sitting still for five minutes, give your mind space to breathe.

5 **Set emotional boundaries.** You are not required to be everyone's sounding board, fixer, therapist or saviour. You can hold space without holding *everything*.

You are more than your productivity.

You are not a machine.

You don't need to earn your rest.

You can manifest a powerful, fulfilling life and still take a break. You can build an empire and still ask for help. You can be strong without being constantly stressed.

Balance isn't about eliminating pressure altogether – it's about building *systems, support and self-awareness* so you're not crushed by it.

Sustainable excellence

Before we move on, I want to return briefly to someone whose invaluable advice and insights we looked at earlier in this chapter – Lewis

Paris, whose work sits at the intersection of movement, mindset and meaningful productivity.

One thing I admire most about Lewis is his emphasis on sustainable excellence. Not the kind that burns bright for a season and fades, but the kind that's built through rhythm, recovery and repeatable habits. As he shared with me: 'High performance isn't about hustle 24/7. It's about understanding when to push and when to pause. It's the combination of exercise and rest that creates the energy, clarity and confidence needed to make real impact.'

That line stayed with me. Because in a world that glorifies constant motion, Lewis reminds us that rest isn't a reward – it's a requirement.

So I asked him: 'What routines or tools can help us build better rhythms, especially when we're trying to juggle big goals with real life?'

Here are a few of Lewis's most powerful insights to help you reset your productivity, protect your energy and optimise your day for long-term success.

Lewis Paris's longevity-inspired productivity habits

1 **Set a consistent wake-up time and build your bedtime around it.** Rather than obsessing over getting to sleep earlier, Lewis suggests starting with a consistent wake-up time, even on weekends. This anchors your circadian rhythm and naturally improves sleep quality over time. You'll start to feel tired earlier, without forcing it.

2 **Delay your coffee by 60–90 minutes.** Yes, really. While it's tempting to reach for caffeine the moment you wake up, Lewis advises holding off to let your body's natural cortisol levels rise first. This prevents afternoon crashes and supports more stable energy throughout the day.

3 **Move your body within 30 minutes of waking.** This doesn't have to be a full workout – it could be 10–15 minutes of mobility drills, a brisk walk or gentle stretching. Movement early in the day helps regulate mood, improve focus and jumpstart your metabolism.

4 **Make your mornings distraction-free.** Lewis empha-
sises doing your 'deep work' first – before the world
has a chance to pull at your attention. No scrolling, no
inbox-diving. Just clear, focused action on your most
important task.

5 **Protect the evening wind-down.** Set a cut-off time for
work and screens, and introduce calming rituals instead –
a hot shower, herbal tea, gentle stretching or journaling.
This signals to your body that it's safe to rest and improves
sleep depth and quality.

6 **Bookend your day with reflection.** Morning journaling helps you clarify intentions and focus. Evening
reflection helps you process your day – wins, lessons and
gratitude. Lewis notes that this 'mental flossing' keeps
your thoughts from spiralling and increases emotional
resilience.

7 **Embrace the power of cold.** Lewis swears by morning
cold showers to stimulate alertness, reduce inflammation
and boost mood. While not for everyone, it's a practice
that builds discipline and gives a mental edge before the
day even begins. (Cold showers are just not something
I have been able to master, but apparently you only need
a short time in the cold to see impact!)

8 **Schedule joy like you would a meeting.** This one
aligns perfectly with everything we've explored in this
chapter. Lewis believes productivity isn't about rigidity –
it's about rhythm. That means making space for creativity,
connection and curiosity. As he puts it, 'If your calendar
has no room for joy, it's not productivity – it's survival.'
(Now this, I can get behind!)

These habits aren't about perfection. They're about pattern.

And in the context of managing stress, pressure and the mental
load, small changes like these can lead to massive shifts in how we
feel, think and show up in the world.

You don't need to copy Lewis's routine exactly, but you can take inspiration from it and build your own. Because when you protect your energy, you amplify your impact.

Understanding the mental load and finding balance across the Five Principles

The truth is, the mental load doesn't show up the same way for everyone. It's shaped by our roles, our responsibilities and the unique rhythm of our lives. That's why I want to revisit the Five Principles of Manifested Action to show how pressure manifests across these domains and how you might begin to lighten the load in each one.

1. CAREER

You might be navigating demanding bosses, tight deadlines or unrealistic expectations – all while trying to progress, upskill or transition roles. The mental load here is the pressure to *perform* while trying to remain *visible*, *strategic* and *valuable*. Add to that office politics or diversity dynamics, and the stress multiplies.

Ask yourself:

- Are you carrying more than your job description requires?
- Have you communicated your bandwidth, or are you quietly overdelivering out of fear of looking incapable?

2. ENTREPRENEURSHIP

Running a business means wearing *every hat* – from visionary to operations to finance to marketing. Your mind rarely switches off, even at 2 a.m. You're the decision-maker, the problem-solver, the leader and often the entire HR department. Stress can feel like your shadow.

Ask yourself:

- Are you doing tasks you could delegate?
- Are you building your dream, or drowning in your to-do list?

3. FAMILY AND RELATIONSHIPS

Whether you're parenting young children, supporting a partner, looking after ageing relatives or maintaining friendships, your emotional and logistical bandwidth is constantly stretched. From remembering birthdays to scheduling dentist appointments, the unpaid labour is *very real.*

Ask yourself:

- Are your family relationships reciprocal, or are you the organiser-in-chief by default?
- Who can you ask to take something off your plate?

4. SELF

This is the one we neglect the most. We put ourselves last, assuming we'll get to it *after everything else.* But ignoring your emotional needs, your rest, your hobbies and your joy doesn't make you more noble. It makes you more depleted.

Ask yourself:

- What are you holding on to out of obligation, not alignment?
- When was the last time you checked in with you?

5. HEALTH

Stress often shows up in the body before it registers in the mind. Burnout, anxiety, sleep disruptions, emotional eating or physical fatigue – these are all signals. If you're not well, everything else falls apart.

Ask yourself:

- Are you creating space for recovery, or only productivity?
- What does your body need right now – and are you listening?

This framework isn't meant to overwhelm you. It's meant to give you a mirror.

To say: *Yes, this is a lot. And no, you don't have to carry it all on your own.*

By recognising where your mental load is heaviest, you can begin to shift, delegate, pause or get support in ways that serve your long-term vision.

Reflection exercise: Building your rhythm, not perfection

If there's one thing I've learned – through building businesses, raising a child, managing a household, and trying to be a decent human being along the way – it's this: there is no perfect formula for balance.

There is no magic planner, no five-step routine, no immaculate to-do list that will give you everything, all at once, in equal measure.

What there *is*, however, is rhythm. Your own rhythm. One that shifts with your seasons. One that honours your capacity. One that leaves space for rest, recovery, resilience and joy.

The goal isn't to 'do it all'. The goal is to do what matters. The goal is to *feel* your way through, not force your way through. To take action in alignment with your vision, while giving yourself permission to pivot when life changes shape.

There will be days when work takes more from you. There will be weeks when your child, your parent or your body needs more from you.

There will be seasons when your goals evolve, but that doesn't mean you've failed. It means you've grown.

You don't have to earn your rest. You don't have to prove your productivity.

You just have to be honest with yourself about what you need, what you want and what you're willing to change to get there.

So, instead of striving for balance like it's some perfectly symmetrical scale, ask yourself this: 'What's the rhythm of the life I want to live – and what's one step I can take this week to honour it?'

Your manifested action steps

As always, this chapter ends not just with reflection, but with *action*. Here are your steps to help you integrate everything you've learned into the next chapter of your life:

- **Audit your energy.** Track your week. What energises you? What drains you? Start making decisions based on energy, not just obligation.
- **Define your boundaries.** Where are you saying 'yes' when you mean 'no'? What's one boundary you can set this week to protect your time, your peace or your priorities?
- **Delegate one thing.** Choose a task that doesn't serve your highest vision and either outsource it, automate it or hand it off. Remember: delegation creates space for elevation.
- **Build in non-negotiable self-care.** Identify one daily habit that supports your wellbeing and protect it. Whether it's a walk, a bath, a stretch or a moment of silence – make it yours.
- **Check your rhythm, not your perfection.** Are you flowing in the direction of your goals? Or are you forcing balance where flexibility would serve you better?

Setting the stage for success

You don't have to 'do it all' to be successful. You just have to do what matters – consistently, intentionally, and with enough compassion to keep going when life inevitably shifts.

Because the truth is, the most powerful version of you is not the one who never drops the ball. It's the one who knows which balls are glass, which are rubber, and which ones you can put down for now and pick back up when you're ready.

Your rhythm is yours to build. Let's honour that – fully.

CHAPTER NINE
Leaving a Legacy

Legacy, to me (Byron), has always transcended personal accolades or the mere accumulation of wealth. It's not about the flash – it's about the footprint. The imprint you leave behind. The ripple effect of your actions, your decisions, your leadership, and the way you choose to show up in the world. It's about the lives you touch – directly and indirectly – and the opportunities you create for others to succeed. That's real legacy.

Now let's pause for a second and break it down.

What is legacy?

By dictionary definition, a legacy is: 'Something transmitted by or received from an ancestor or predecessor from the past.'[1]

But in the real world, legacy is about so much more than what you leave behind when you're gone – it's about what you *give* while you're here. It's not just the inheritance you pass on in the form of money, property or titles. It's the influence. The insight. The inspiration. It's what you embed in people, systems, communities and industries.

Of course, for many of us, legacy starts with our children. And rightly so. Becoming a father changed my entire perspective. There is something sacred about looking into the eyes of the next generation and thinking, 'What am I leaving for you? What am I modelling for you?' But legacy isn't only about parenting. Some of the greatest leg-acies the world has ever known were created by people who poured their wisdom, energy and resources into communities, causes, busi-nesses and movements that reshaped the world.

So whether or not you have children, your life still has the power to plant seeds that grow into trees you may never sit under. Legacy is a mindset. It's a commitment to contribution. It's the belief that you are not just here to *exist* – you are here to *build*.

Throughout our journey, Bianca and I have been privileged to mentor over a thousand entrepreneurs, guiding many of them to achieve six- and seven-figure successes. We've published books that have touched the lives of tens of thousands of readers around the world. Every review, every email from a mentee, every message that starts with, 'I followed your advice, and now . . .' – that's legacy in motion. That's when you know the work is working.

We've always believed that our impact would outlive us. But what we didn't anticipate was how quickly that legacy would evolve. After 14 years of supporting Bianca in the speaking industry – watching her move audiences, influence decision-makers and redefine the value of a voice – we began to notice a pattern: too many speakers had incredible stories, insights and knowledge to share, but no idea how to communicate that value effectively. Even worse, they were doing it all for free.

Now don't get me wrong, volunteering is noble. But speaking for free at every event, without strategy, structure or end-goal? That's not sustainable. And frankly, it damages the industry and people's pockets.

So we created something we knew was missing: the Self Made Speaking Academy. A two-day immersive training experience to help career professionals and entrepreneurs alike find their voice, define their niche, build their personal brand, master the art of storytelling, understand the business of speaking and – importantly – get paid.

To date, we've trained hundreds of speakers. Many of them now command £4,000 –£10,000 for a single 20-minute keynote. Why? Because they know how to position themselves, market themselves and *ask* for what they're worth. We've helped mentees walk away with full confidence that they deserve to be compensated for the value they bring – and companies are paying them accordingly.

That, to me, is legacy.

But it doesn't stop there. As our lives evolve, so does our mission. We've now set our sights on creating 1,000 paid professional speakers within the next two years. Ambitious? Yes. Possible? Absolutely. We've built the blueprint – we just need the voices.

Let's be clear about the opportunity. The speaking industry is powerful and profitable. In the UK, keynote speakers typically earn between £2,000 and £20,000 per engagement, depending on profile, experience and client. In the US, the average speaking fee starts around $2,500, with top-tier professionals earning $30,000-plus for a single talk. This isn't a side hustle – it's a thriving industry.

And because we believe in keeping the pipeline open, we've launched our own speaker agency to represent some of our alumni. That means we're not just teaching speakers how to market themselves; we're also giving them the platform to be seen, hired and booked by some of the most prestigious companies in the world.

When people talk about being 'self-made', they often assume it means doing everything on your own. But our legacy has been built in *supporting others* to become self-made in their own right. In every entrepreneur we've mentored, every mentee we've empowered, every speaker we've trained, we see our legacy reflected back to us.

That is what this chapter is about: creating something that outlives you, outgrows you and continues to serve long after your name leaves the room.

Defining your legacy – values, vision and mission

Let's start with the truth: legacy isn't built by accident.

It's crafted – consciously and consistently – by people who know what they stand for and where they're headed.

That means your legacy begins with values, is shaped by your vision and is delivered through your mission.

Without these, you're just moving – possibly fast – without direction.

VALUES: WHAT YOU STAND FOR

Your values are your foundation. They're the compass behind every decision you make and every action you take.
Ask yourself:

- What matters to me more than anything else?
- What will I not compromise on, even if no one is watching?
- What do I want people to experience when they interact with me or my work?

For Bianca and me, our values have always included impact, integrity and empowerment. We don't just want to win – we want to see others win *with us*, and often *because of us*. That's reflected in how we coach, how we serve and how we lead.

VISION: WHERE YOU'RE GOING

Your vision is the future you're building.
It's the world you want to help create – not just for yourself, but for your family, your community and beyond.
Your vision isn't limited to your income goals or your business size.
It's about legacy in motion: the *feeling* people get from your brand, the way you shift the culture in your workplace, or the way your children grow up understanding that they are limitless.
Think of your vision like a north star.
It won't give you every step, but it will keep you heading in the right direction when distractions try to pull you off course.

MISSION: HOW YOU'RE GOING TO GET THERE

Your mission is where your values and vision get operationalised.
It's the 'what' and the 'how' behind your everyday decisions.
It's not a paragraph for your website. It's the driver behind the way you show up in meetings, how you treat your team, how you run your household, how you speak on stage, how you negotiate deals and how you serve your community.

You don't have to have a perfect mission statement, but you do need a clear sense of how your daily actions align with what you ultimately want to be remembered for.

Legacy through action – giving, building, lifting

There's a phrase we use often in the world of entrepreneurship: 'Show me your calendar, and I'll show you your values.'

I'd take it one step further: 'Show me where your time, money and energy go, and I'll show you your legacy.'

Legacy isn't built in your head. It's built in your hands.

It's not found in ideas alone – it's found in *action*.

The truth is, many people talk about legacy like it's some distant concept, something to worry about once you've hit a certain net worth or entered retirement. But the people who create real impact – the ones who leave behind something meaningful – understand that legacy is a *daily practice*. It's in what you choose to prioritise, who you choose to uplift, and how you choose to give, even when no one's watching.

At its heart, legacy is about building beyond yourself.

Legacy in the choice to give

I've never been afraid to enjoy the finer things in life. Anyone who knows me will tell you that I love celebrating wins – I've had some unforgettable birthdays over the years. Lavish parties, tailored suits, incredible venues, surrounded by good people and good energy. There's nothing wrong with enjoying the fruits of your labour. But as the years go on, and especially since becoming a father, I've started to think more deeply about how those celebrations can serve a greater purpose.

This year, I made a different kind of choice.

Instead of planning another extravagant event, I decided to dedicate my birthday to something that would create genuine impact. I asked our network – friends, family, clients, mentees – to *donate instead of gifting*. No cards. No bottles. No big night out. Just one ask: help us raise money for a local soup kitchen to feed and care for the homeless.

And the response? Phenomenal.

Together, we raised thousands of pounds, which went directly towards:

- preparing and serving more than 100 hot meals
- distributing sleeping bags, toiletries, warm clothing and other essentials
- creating care packs with dignity items many of us take for granted
- showing real love to people who are often invisible in our communities

There was no PR stunt. No press release. Just people coming together to make a difference. And for me, it was one of the most fulfilling ways I've ever spent a birthday. Not because I got anything in return, but because I knew that, *somewhere*, someone was warmer, fed and seen – because we showed up.

That is legacy. Not the spotlight. Not the accolades.

But the act of being useful, human and generous – even when you know your name may never be remembered by the person you helped.

The myth that you need millions to make an impact

Let's debunk something here: legacy is *not* reserved for billionaires. You don't need a charitable foundation or a viral campaign to start building your legacy through action.

You need awareness. You need intent. And you need to stop waiting until you've 'made it' to start making a difference.

Some of the greatest legacy-makers are people whose names will never trend, but whose fingerprints are all over the lives of those around them:

- the coach who mentored generations of young people, helping them believe in their ability to succeed
- the nurse who went above and beyond in every interaction, treating strangers with dignity when no one else would
- the small business owner who always hired local, trained up staff, and gave second chances when others wouldn't

None of them had trust funds or television deals. But all of them built legacy through consistent, compassionate action.

Lifting as you climb

Whether it's financial giving, mentorship, community work or creating opportunities for others, legacy is built every time you use your power to uplift someone else.

And don't be fooled – *you do have power.* Even if you're not a millionaire. Even if your business is still growing. Even if you're still figuring it all out. You have a voice. You have time. You have experiences that can help someone else shorten their learning curve or soften their landing.

Every time you share knowledge, pass on a contact, mentor someone new, or say someone's name in a room they haven't yet entered, you're creating legacy.

Examples of legacy in action

Let's look at some real-world examples of legacy through action.

- **Marcus Rashford**, the British footballer, used his platform to fight child food poverty and ensure free school meals were provided for vulnerable children in the UK. He didn't just post – he partnered, he pushed policies, he persisted. That's legacy in action.
- **Melinda French Gates**, through the Bill & Melinda Gates Foundation, has contributed billions to health, education and gender equity – supporting the lives of people she'll never meet.
- **Local entrepreneurs** in your own community who create jobs, mentor youth, fundraise for causes or provide free services during hardship. This is the less-publicised, deeply powerful side of legacy that doesn't make headlines but does change lives.

Creating legacy at scale

As much as legacy is built through individual moments – through giving your time, showing up for others and acting with intention – it can also be multiplied when you create a system that helps others do the same.

That's something Bianca and I have become incredibly passionate about in recent years: building platforms that enable other people to build *their own* legacy. Not just making an impact ourselves, but creating vehicles through which others can share their stories, access their power and step into their purpose.

The Self Made Speaking Academy is one of the clearest examples of that mission. But what excites us most isn't just that people are now commanding four-figure speaking fees. It's that they're finally taking up space. They're finally being *heard*.

We're seeing people move from undervalued and overlooked to *booked and respected* – sharing their expertise in boardrooms, at conferences and on stages they once thought were out of reach. And, in doing so, they're influencing others, changing minds, shifting culture and building wealth. That's legacy on a loop.

It's not about us. It's about the ripple effect.

That's what creating legacy at scale looks like:

- It's not just mentoring one person – it's building a model that empowers hundreds.
- It's not just speaking to an audience – it's creating more speakers with their own audiences.
- It's not just being the expert – it's helping others become experts in their own right.

Legacy multiplies when you move from being the star of the show to being the producer of many shows.

And that's the kind of work that lives on long after the applause fades.

Reflection exercise: What are you building for others?

So, here's the real question: who will thank you years from now for something you did today?

- Will it be the young mentee who got their first opportunity because you vouched for them?
- Will it be the single parent who launched their side hustle after you gave them advice over coffee?
- Will it be the community member whose life changed because of a resource, a connection or a contribution you made?

These are the building blocks of legacy.

Legacy doesn't have to be loud. But it does have to be deliberate.

And it doesn't start 'one day' down the line. It starts *today* – with what you choose to give, build and lift.

Ask yourself: what are you building for others?

Legacy isn't just about what you create – it's about who you help rise because of what you created.

- Are you lifting people as you climb?
- Are you making your corner of the world better?
- Are you choosing to give even when it would be easier not to?

You don't need a foundation to be a force for good. You just need to act – with intention, with heart and with consistency.

Building a legacy business or brand

There's a big difference between building something that makes money and building something that makes meaning. And if there's one thing I've learned over the past two decades in business, it's that you can't build a true legacy on hustle alone.

Anyone can start a business. Many can make it profitable. But building something that lasts? Something that serves people beyond your reach, that outlives your day-to-day involvement, that represents something bigger than you? That takes a different level of intention.

For me, legacy in business has always been about depth, not just scale. It's not just about how many people know your name; it's about what your name means to those who do.

We often romanticise the idea of being 'self-made', and while our first book proudly carried that title, we've always been clear: being self-made doesn't mean being entirely self-sufficient. Legacy isn't created in a vacuum. It's created through service, collaboration and consistency. It's the product of thousands of decisions – some strategic, some instinctive and some, quite frankly, sacrificial.

The businesses Bianca and I have built were never designed just to put money in our pockets. Yes, they generate income, but, more importantly, they create opportunity. They empower others. They unlock potential. They provide jobs, shift mindsets and serve our clients in ways that help them build legacies of their own.

That's the part many miss when they talk about entrepreneurship. It's not just about being your own boss – it's about being a builder of systems, culture and impact. A legacy business is one that, even if your name disappears from the paperwork, your principles, standards and intention remain embedded in every corner.

Legacy is found in the way you build

One of the hardest lessons to learn in business is that being busy isn't the same as being effective. In the early years of growing one of my service-based companies, the diary was full. The team was out working non-stop. On paper, we looked successful. But when I sat down to really review the numbers, something didn't add up. The revenue wasn't reflecting the effort.

As I stated (courtesy of my father-in-law) in Chapter 5, 'Don't be a busy fool.'

We were working hard, but not necessarily working smart. The business had grown, but the model hadn't adapted. We were reacting, not leading. And it reminded me that legacy doesn't live in chaos – it lives in *clarity*. It lives in how you align your daily actions with the bigger picture you're trying to build.

That's the shift every founder has to make at some point: from being inside the machine to stepping outside and asking, 'Is this machine even doing what I built it for?'

What about career professionals?

Now, if you're reading this and thinking, 'Well, I'm not running a business', let me say this clearly: you still have a legacy to build.

Whether you're in education, finance, healthcare, law, tech, retail – whatever your profession – your legacy is in how you lead, how you support others, how you innovate, and how you leave things better than you found them.

A legacy career isn't about climbing the ladder the fastest; it's about lifting others as you climb. It's about becoming the kind of colleague people remember for all the right reasons. The one who mentored the intern, challenged the culture, opened the door for someone else. That's leadership. And leadership is legacy.

Building with others in mind

When I think about the businesses we've built, what I'm most proud of isn't the awards or the accolades. It's the people. The team members who joined us early on and now manage others in the team. The mentees who went from idea to thriving business. The speakers who now command thousands per keynote and are changing lives with their messages. That's where the legacy lives.

And as a husband, father and founder, I'm constantly asking myself: what am I embedding into this business that Ethan will be proud of? What systems will still work if I take a step back? Who else gets better because of what we've built?

It's easy to get caught up in day-to-day survival mode. But legacy reminds us to zoom out. To ask the bigger questions. To make decisions with the next generation in mind – not just the next quarter.

You don't have to be famous to build a legacy brand.

You don't need a million followers.

What you need is vision, values and the discipline to show up with purpose, over and over again.

Because one day, someone will stand on the foundation you laid, and they'll either thrive or struggle, depending on the integrity of your work.

Let's make sure they thrive.

Measuring impact – what does your legacy look like in real life?

One of the most humbling and grounding moments in this journey of building businesses, mentoring entrepreneurs and shaping programmes is when someone – often a stranger – approaches you and tells you that your work changed something for them. It could be a sentence they read in a book, a comment we made during a masterclass, a resource we recommended, or even just the way we showed up in a moment. What's fascinating is that you don't always know the ripple effect of what you're doing until it reaches you in ways you hadn't anticipated.

You see, we often think of legacy as this grand finale – a moment when the curtain rises for the final time and people applaud what you've built. But the reality is that legacy isn't found in the big reveals. It lives in the quiet shifts, the small acknowledgements, and the lasting impressions you've left behind that continue to shape the world long after the meeting ends, the call finishes or the event wraps up.

I've had mentees reach out months or even years after we last spoke to tell me they've finally launched their business, doubled their income, or walked away from something that no longer served them because of something they heard us say. I've received messages from people I've never met who read our books during a low point in their lives and used them as a roadmap to rebuild. That's legacy. Not necessarily visible. Not always immediate. But deeply real.

Legacy isn't always loud – but it's always lasting

Legacy doesn't always roar – it often whispers.

It shows up in a mentee's confidence when they pitch for a deal. It's in the shift in mindset of someone who once believed they were stuck and now knows they have options. It's in the junior staff member who felt safe enough to bring new ideas forward because the environment we created encouraged innovation.

And it's in the culture of our team – the standards we uphold, the conversations we're willing to have, and the boundaries we set to protect what we've built. These things don't make headlines, but they matter. Because the truth is, most of us won't have statues built in our name. But the way we make people feel, the tools we give them, the belief we pass on – that's where legacy lives.

It's easy to assume that legacy only comes with scale or status, but that's not the case. Whether you're leading a team of one or one hundred, writing policy or poetry, hosting global conferences or reading bedtime stories – your impact matters. You're shaping something. And every day is an opportunity to be intentional about what that something becomes.

How do you know it's working?

It's a valid question. One I've asked myself many times.

How do you know if what you're doing is landing the way you hope? How do you measure your impact if the feedback isn't always instant or tangible?

You start by looking around. Really looking.

- Do the people you lead grow under your leadership?
- Do your clients get results, feel empowered or shift their mindset after working with you?
- Are you creating environments where others can win, not just you?
- Do people come back – not because they have to, but because they want to?

And then you look inward:

- Are your values intact?
- Is the way you're working in alignment with the bigger vision you say you're working toward?
- Do you sleep well at night knowing that your name and your work represent integrity, excellence and service?

If the answer is yes – even quietly, even inconsistently – you're already building legacy.

Legacy is the sum of your everyday choices

There's a powerful misconception that legacy happens all at once – that there will be this moment where, suddenly, your impact is undeniable and the world stops to acknowledge it. But, in truth, legacy is shaped by the choices we make every single day, especially the ones that no one sees.

It's in how you treat the people who can do nothing for you.

It's in how you show up when the money isn't flowing or the results haven't come yet.

It's in whether you choose growth over comfort, accountability over ego, and community over competition.

Sometimes legacy looks like a mentoring programme.

Sometimes it looks like feeding the homeless instead of throwing a birthday party.

Sometimes it looks like a kind word at the right moment that helps someone keep going.

None of it is wasted. None of it is too small.

A reminder for when it feels slow

There will be seasons when your legacy doesn't feel visible.

When the clients are quiet, the feedback is low, and the work feels like it's happening in a vacuum. In those moments, it's easy to feel like none of it matters. Like your time, your energy, your generosity is going unnoticed.

Don't stop.

Some people won't acknowledge your impact until they need you again.
Some won't realise your value until you're no longer available.
Some will never tell you that you changed their life, but they'll change someone else's because of it.

And that counts.

Impact you can feel

So, if you're wondering what your legacy looks like in real life, start small.

Look at your team. Your family. Your clients. Your community.

Look at the environments you've shaped, the energy you bring, the standard you set.

You might be making more of a difference than you realise. And if not yet, then you start now – by asking yourself not just what you can *do*, but what you can *leave behind* in the process.

Because legacy isn't something you build later. It's something you're already building now.

Legacy through the lens of the Five Principles

Let's take this a step further. Legacy isn't built in one area of life.

It touches everything – your career, your business, your family, your health, your personal growth. That's why we return again to the Five Principles of Manifested Action.

Let's break down how legacy looks in each.

1. CAREER

Your legacy isn't just your LinkedIn profile or your job title. It's how you led meetings, how you mentored junior colleagues, how you created opportunities for others to grow. It's the ripple effect of your presence in the workplace.

Ask yourself:

- Am I mentoring or supporting anyone in my organisation?
- What do I want people to say about me when I leave a role?

2. ENTREPRENEURSHIP

If you're building a business, you're also building a system. That system can uplift people, or it can exploit them. A legacy-driven entrepreneur builds something that makes money, yes, but also *makes a difference*.

Ask yourself:

- Is my business solving a real problem?
- Am I proud of the way we treat people – clients, customers, staff?

3. FAMILY AND RELATIONSHIPS

Legacy here isn't just inheritance – it's modelling.

Your values, your habits, your self-worth, your emotional literacy – all of that becomes the blueprint for what your children or loved ones believe is possible.

Ask yourself:

- What unspoken lessons am I teaching through my actions?
- What do I want to pass down, beyond money or material goods?

4. SELF

Legacy also lives in how you speak to yourself.

It's the habits you choose. The standards you keep. The boundaries you honour. How you treat yourself sets the tone for how the world treats you.

Ask yourself:

- Am I living in a way that aligns with who I say I want to be?
- What limiting behaviours or beliefs am I passing down without realising?

5. HEALTH

A legacy of longevity, vitality and rest is powerful. You're not just staying alive – you're showing others what it looks like to *live well*.
Ask yourself:

- Do I take care of my body and mind like they're part of my future legacy?
- Am I modelling sustainable energy, or glorifying burnout?

When you define your values, vision and mission – *across* these five areas – you begin to shape a life of depth and direction.

A life that isn't just about what you accumulate, but what you *activate* in the world around you.

Your legacy starts with a decision: to live on purpose, every single day.

Reflection exercise: Your legacy is already under construction

Here's the truth: whether you've been aware of it or not, you've already started building your legacy.

Every decision you've made – every challenge you've overcome, every time you've chosen to act with integrity, every moment you've invested in someone else's growth – has been part of the foundation. And the beauty is, you don't need to have it all figured out before you begin shaping something powerful.

Legacy isn't just about what you leave *after* you're gone.

It's about what you contribute while you're here.
It's in your ideas, your voice, your relationships, your impact.
You don't need to be famous to be remembered.

173

You don't need to be a billionaire to be a blessing. You simply need to be intentional.

As you reflect on the journey of this book – from defining your vision to taking consistent action, navigating fear, building resilience, and now stepping into your legacy – remember this:

You are capable of building something that lasts. Something that matters. Something that reflects the best of who you are.

Your manifested legacy plan: Action steps

Let's end this chapter the way we end every one – by taking what's conceptual and turning it into committed action. Here are your legacy prompts. Don't rush them. Sit with them. Write them down. Let them guide your next season of growth.

- **Define your legacy intention.** What do you want people to say about your impact, years from now? Think beyond titles and achievements – what values do you want to be known for?
- **Audit your influence.** Look at your career, business, community and home. Where are you already making an impact, and where could you go deeper?
- **Create a legacy action list.** Choose three tangible ways to build your legacy this year. It could be mentoring someone, launching a community initiative, writing that book, or setting up your systems to thrive without you.
- **Share the vision.** Who needs to know about your legacy plan? Whether it's your team, your family, your co-founder or your coach, bring them in. Legacy is rarely built alone.
- **Commit to long-term consistency.** Remember, legacy is the result of sustained action. What habits, disciplines or boundaries do you need to establish to stay on course?

This isn't the end of your journey. It's the beginning of a new chapter – one built with purpose, fuelled by action and driven by a vision of something far greater than personal gain.

You've manifested the dream.

Now you're building the reality.

And soon, you'll leave a legacy that outlives you.

We'll be cheering you on – every step of the way.

Setting the stage for success

Legacy isn't built in the distant future – it's shaped by the choices you make today.

Not just the big, public wins, but the quiet decisions to give, to build, to uplift – even when no one's watching.

So ask yourself: what am I creating that will outlive me?

Who will thrive because I chose to show up?

You don't need a title to lead or a million followers to make an impact.

You just need clarity, consistency and the courage to build something that matters – again and again.

Let today be part of your legacy.

CHAPTER TEN
Turning Positive Affirmations into Reality

Feel it first – from words to reality

One thing I (Bianca) always say – especially when I'm working with clients on building their personal brand – is that it's not just about the story you tell the world, it's also about the story you tell *yourself*. And let's be honest, many of us are kinder and more affirming to our friends, our partners and even strangers on the internet than we are to ourselves.

We'll tell a friend she's beautiful. That she deserves the promotion. That she's an amazing mother. We'll cheer her on, send her the link to the job application, help her practise for the interview, repost her business launch like it's our own. But then, we'll look in the mirror and tear ourselves down with the same breath. We'll shrink our dreams with silent doubt. Why?

It's time we held ourselves in the same light we hold others. Affirmations can help us do that – but not if we're just repeating them like a line from a script we've not rehearsed properly. You have to feel it before you can live it. You have to mean what you say. And then – you have to move like you mean it.

Affirming that you're wealthy, successful, confident or loved isn't just about saying it. It's about placing yourself in spaces that reflect it back to you. It's about connecting with the feeling of what that success actually looks and feels like in your body, in your behaviour and in your life.

**You want a certain piece of clothing? Go to the store.
Try it on.
You want to drive a particular car? Book the test drive.
You've written: 'I will own a home'? Book the viewing.
Walk through the space. Stand on the doorstep. Feel
the doorknob in your hand.**

Why? Because that's what it means to move an affirmation from *abstract* to *actual*.

I remember once hearing a coach say that manifestation doesn't work if you're just 'wishing with your eyes closed'. You've got to look your dream in the face and then put yourself in a position to claim it.

You must believe it to build it

In my line of work, helping entrepreneurs and professionals craft strong, authentic personal brands, I've seen first-hand how much power there is in self-belief. When a client walks into a meeting unsure of their value, you can feel it. And, unfortunately, so can everyone else.

One of the first things I say is this: *if you don't believe your story, how can anyone else?*

You are your first audience. And your most important one.

If your internal monologue is telling you you're not good enough, not ready, not worthy, you'll hold back, even when opportunities are right in front of you. You'll shrink, you'll self-sabotage, and you'll settle for less than you deserve.

That's why affirmations, when they're honest and intentional, are so transformative. They're not about pretending. They're about *reminding*. Reminding yourself of your truth, of your potential, of your right to take up space.

Parenting with affirmation – speaking life early

Now, let me bring this into my most personal role yet – being a mother. From the moment my son was born, I've been speaking life into him. Telling him he is kind. That he is intelligent. That he is brave. That he can achieve anything he sets his mind to. Not because he needs to perform for me, but because I want those truths embedded in his subconscious from day one.

Even before he can talk, I believe that his little ears can hear it. That his spirit can absorb it. And now, every time I say, 'You are so clever,' or, 'You're such a good boy,' I imagine that one day, he'll say it too – not just because he's repeating me, but because *he believes it about himself.*

That, to me, is the foundation of self-esteem. That's legacy. That's how you plant affirmations deep enough to grow.

But, of course, I won't stop there. I'll also teach him what action looks like. That being kind means doing kind things. That being smart means being curious, asking questions, trying again when you get it wrong. Because affirmations aren't a free pass – they're a *framework* for how we show up.

Living your affirmation

So, here's the question I want you to consider as you read this chapter: are you living your affirmations, or just reciting them?

You can write 'I am confident' in your journal 300 times, but if you avoid putting your hand up in meetings, if you don't advocate for yourself when it matters, if you never take the risk – you're not living in alignment with that affirmation.

You don't have to have it all figured out. But you do have to act. You do have to show up. Even if it's messy. Even if your voice shakes. Even if the belief comes *after* the step you take.

That's what this chapter – and this life – is really about.

Affirmations and identity – rewiring your inner narrative

I often say to clients that building your personal brand isn't just about the glossy photos, the LinkedIn bio or the polished pitch – it's about understanding and owning your story. And not just the story you *show* to the world, but the one you *tell yourself* when no one else is watching.

That inner narrative? That's what informs everything.

It influences how you walk into a room, how you respond to opportunity, how you recover from failure – and, ultimately, how much of your own potential you allow yourself to access.

This is why affirmations are so powerful, but only when they're integrated into your *identity*. Not just wishful words on paper, but statements that align with your actions, your intentions and your truth. Because here's the reality: you will never outperform your internal belief system. You may fake it for a bit, but eventually your subconscious will pull you back to the level of what you really believe about yourself.

Your story is your strategy

One of the exercises I guide clients through when we're clarifying their brand or planning their next chapter is a simple but powerful framework that helps them take stock of their narrative.

It involves looking at your story in three parts:

1 **Your past** – what have you done?
   ● What moments have shaped you?
   ● What skills have you built, what challenges have you overcome, and what experiences have brought you to where you are today?
2 **Your present** – what are you doing now?
   ● What actions are you taking daily, weekly, consistently?
   ● How are you showing up?
   ● Are you aligned with the goals you say you want?
   ● Are you planting seeds or standing still?
3 **Your future** – what are you willing to do to get where you want to go?
   ● What bold decisions are you ready to make?
   ● What habits need to change?
   ● Who do you need to become in order to step into your next level?

This simple reflection helps people connect the dots between who they say they are, what they've lived through, and where they want to be. It turns vague affirmations into intentional self-awareness.

It uncovers the contradictions and gives people the clarity to create new alignment between their identity and their aspirations.

Your story has to make sense to you first

Because here's what I've seen too often – people repeat affirmations that don't match the story they're actually living.

They'll say, 'I'm building generational wealth,' but they're not reviewing their finances, not investing, not learning.

They'll say, 'I'm an expert in my field,' but their confidence wobbles anytime they're challenged.

They'll say, 'I am enough,' but their decisions are laced with people-pleasing and perfectionism.

When your words and your actions aren't in sync, the world gets confused. And so do you.

Affirmations aren't meant to mask reality. They're meant to help you reshape it. But you can reshape only what you're willing to look at honestly.

So, if your affirmation is, 'I am successful,' the question becomes: *what would a successful person do this week?* What choices would they make? How would they speak? Who would they surround themselves with?

If your affirmation is, 'I am confident,' ask yourself: *what would confidence look like on a Tuesday afternoon when things aren't going to plan?*

When your affirmations are built on top of an honest self-narrative, they stop being fluff and start becoming fuel. They remind you of what's possible and challenge you to act in alignment with the identity you're creating – not just the one you've been living.

Reflection exercise: Rewrite your story

If you're reading this and feeling that internal nudge – that slight discomfort that says, 'There's more I could be doing, more I could be saying, more I could be believing' – good. That's where the shift begins.

Take some time to do this reflection here or in your journal or digital notes:

1 **What are five significant events, experiences or accomplishments from your past that have shaped you?**

    • _____

    • _____

    • _____

    • _____

    • _____

2 **What does your present routine, attitude and environment say about where you are right now?**

    _____

    _____

    _____

3 **And, looking ahead, what are you genuinely willing to do to step into your vision?**

    _____

    _____

    _____

4 **Once you've answered those, write an affirmation that reflects where you're going – not where you've been stuck.**

    _____

    _____

    _____

5 **Then ask: what's one action I can take this week to reinforce this affirmation with real behaviour?**

_____

_____

_____

This is how you turn a story into a strategy.
  This is how you build belief.
  And this is how affirmations stop being a whisper and start becoming your reality.

From intention to execution – planning for manifestation

You can have all the clarity in the world – affirmations stuck on your mirror, a vision board filled with all your heart's desires, journal entries for days – but, at some point, the rubber has to hit the road. Because clarity without execution is just daydreaming. And execution without clarity? That's just hustle without direction.

Manifestation is most powerful when it's backed by _intention_. But intention must be followed by _execution_. That means action. Real, structured, imperfect, consistent action. Not just busywork. Not just reacting to the chaos of your inbox. But deliberate movement that aligns with your desired outcome.

In my experience, the most successful people aren't just dreamers; they're _doers_ with a system. They take the words 'I am . . .' and follow them with a plan: 'So I will . . .'

Reverse-engineer your affirmation

Let's say your affirmation is: 'I am a confident public speaker.' Well, then let's work backwards from that. What does a confident speaker do?

- They join a training programme or attend workshops (Self Made Speaking Academy obviously, haha).
- They decide what their expert topic is.
- They practise.
- They record themselves and refine their delivery.
- They take up speaking opportunities.
- They invest in their personal brand so that when they speak, people *listen*.

Suddenly, that single line becomes a strategy. It becomes a lifestyle. It becomes a calendar of tasks that make the affirmation *real*.

This is how I coach my clients – not just to speak life into their goals, but to *breathe movement into them*. Your affirmations should leave footprints. We should be able to trace your progress back to the beliefs you hold about yourself.

Break it down. Build it up

If you've ever stood at the bottom of a mountain of ambition, you'll know that overwhelm is real. That's why I'm a big believer in chunking goals into actionable steps.

You want to build a six-figure business? Let's not just affirm it – let's break it down:

- What product or service are you offering?
- Who is your ideal client?
- What's your pricing model?
- How many sales do you need to hit your first milestone?
- What platform or visibility strategy are you using?

Suddenly, the affirmation 'I am a successful entrepreneur' isn't floating in the clouds – it's grounded in process. In decisions. In habits.

Whether your goal is to write a book, improve your health, get a promotion or relocate your family, the approach is the same. You take the dream and you turn it into a system of behaviour. Your affirmation becomes a compass, and your strategy becomes the map.

Staying the course with positive self-talk

Let's get something straight: positive self-talk isn't wishy-washy. It's neuroscience.

We're not talking about manifesting by sitting cross-legged and hoping the universe drops your dream job into your lap. What we're talking about is one of the most powerful psychological tools available to every single one of us – *if we're willing to use it.*

I've spoken to hundreds of people – corporate professionals, creatives, entrepreneurs – who initially wrote off positive affirmations and self-talk as 'a bit too fluffy for me'. And I get it. We've all seen the overly glamorised version of manifestation online – set to ambient music, accompanied by a voiceover telling you that you are a golden light of cosmic energy (no offence if that's your vibe, by the way).

Let's be honest, affirmations feel amazing when you're winning.

When the opportunities are flowing, your inbox is full of good news, your skin's glowing and your bank balance is smiling – it's easy to say things like, 'I am powerful,' or, 'I attract abundance.' But the true power of positive self-talk isn't about making a good day better. It's about *getting through* the hard days without losing sight of who you are and where you're going.

You know the ones I mean – the days when nothing seems to go right. When you second-guess your decision to leave that job, start that business, write that book, pitch that idea. The moments when things are quiet. Or disappointing. Or slow.

That's when the voice in your head gets louder.

And it's either cheering you on – or quietly dismantling your confidence, one sentence at a time.

Your brain believes what you tell it – that's neuroplasticity

Here's what cuts through the fluff: science. Hard evidence. Real transformation.

Let's talk about the brain.

There's a phenomenon called neuroplasticity – the brain's ability to rewire itself based on repeated thoughts, actions and experiences. This is not an Instagram quote. This is decades of peer-reviewed research.

The more you repeat a thought – positive or negative – the stronger the neural pathway becomes. It's like walking the same path in a field over and over again. Eventually, that path becomes a road. Then a highway. Then your automatic go-to.

So when you repeatedly tell yourself, 'I always mess this up,' or, 'I'm not good with money,' or, 'I'm not confident enough to lead' – your brain believes it. It files it under 'truth' and begins scanning your environment for evidence to support it. It even starts filtering out any contradictory information. That's how powerful your self-talk is.

But flip it – and the reverse becomes true. Tell yourself, 'I am capable. I can figure this out. I've done hard things before.' And guess what? Your brain adapts. It rewires. It builds new neural pathways that reinforce confidence, resilience and belief.

The science of self-talk in practice

Let's look at the research.

A study published in *Social Cognitive and Affective Neuroscience* showed that self-affirmation activates the brain's reward centres, particularly in the ventromedial prefrontal cortex.[1] This is the same area activated by things like chocolate or social connection – things that make us feel *good*, safe and strong.

A meta study in the *Journal of Sport and Exercise Psychology* showed that athletes who used positive self-talk performed significantly better under pressure than those who didn't.[2] And this isn't just for sports – this same principle applies to public speaking, high-stakes meetings, parenting, business launches . . . you name it.

Why? Because self-talk can literally lower cortisol (your stress hormone), regulate your nervous system, and sharpen your ability to focus.

Put simply: positive self-talk is a mental performance enhancer.

Self-talk is not just a tool – it's a lifeline

In those moments, positive self-talk is not fluffy. It's essential. It becomes the lifeline that pulls you back to centre when your circumstances make you feel unworthy, overwhelmed or off course.

And the key to making it work is this: your self-talk must be anchored in truth, not perfection.

You don't need to lie to yourself. You don't need to pretend everything is fine. But you *do* need to remind yourself:

- You've overcome before.
- You are growing, even if you can't see it yet.
- You are allowed to be in progress and still believe in the outcome.

Let me give you a real-life example. When we were preparing for the launch of our second book, *The Business Survival Kit*, we'd already experienced the highs and lessons of publishing our first. But that didn't stop the pressure from building. We'd set a goal to hit the *Sunday Times* Bestsellers List, and that came with all kinds of fears – *What if we don't hit it? What if the strategy fails? What if people don't show up for us?*

And, on those days, I had to remind myself: *I am not starting from scratch. I am building on a foundation that is already solid. I know who I am. I know the value of what we've created. And I know how to show up, even when I'm unsure of the outcome.*

That's what positive self-talk does. It realigns you with your truth when fear tries to distort the view.

So why does it still sound like nonsense to some people?

Because it's simple. And we often undervalue simple.

We've been conditioned to believe that change has to be hard, or that tools must be complex to be credible. But as someone who's lived a life powered by both mindset *and* strategy, I can tell you: *the most effective tools are often the most accessible.*

You don't need fancy apps, a £5k mastermind, or a personal coach whispering in your ear 24/7 (although, if you want that, you know where to find us). You need consistent, empowered language that supports the identity you're building.

Try this when the doubt creeps in

Let's say you've had a day:

- The client said no.
- The pitch flopped.
- The kids are screaming.
- You feel behind.

Pause.
Breathe.
Say: 'I am allowed to feel overwhelmed, but I'm also equipped to figure this out.'

You've just disrupted the spiral. You've shifted your perspective. You've activated the part of your brain that seeks solutions instead of shutdown. That is not fluff. That is *function*.

Here are some more examples of what I encourage clients to say when the inner critic starts playing up to shift their energy in real time:

- 'This feels difficult, but I've done difficult things before.'
- 'I may not have all the answers today, but I'm smart enough to figure it out.'
- 'I don't need everyone to believe in me. I need to believe in me.'
- 'Delay doesn't mean denial.'
- 'I'm still becoming the person who can hold the vision.'

And when things really wobble, go back to something simple, something grounding: 'I am still here. I am still standing. And that counts for something.'

Still not convinced? Let's talk real results

Oprah, Serena Williams, Tom Daley, Michelle Obama – these are people who have publicly credited positive mindset, visualisation and self-belief as essential components of their success. None of them say, 'I waited to believe in myself until everyone else did.' They believed *first*, acted accordingly and the world caught up.

And for me? I can honestly say that the self-talk I practised when no one knew my name was just as important as the speeches I've given on global stages since. That voice inside – that script I was constantly editing and upgrading – *that's what kept me showing up.*

The compelling case for trying this (even if you're sceptical)

Here's what I'd say if you've always rolled your eyes at this stuff: you already talk to yourself.

The question is: *what's the quality of that conversation?*

Is it nourishing you or wearing you down? Is it moving you forward or pulling you back? You don't need to believe in magic. You just need to believe in *agency* – your ability to influence your thoughts, and therefore your choices, and therefore your outcomes.

You've got the tool.

Now it's time to use it intentionally.

How to build a habit of positive self-talk

If this isn't your natural default yet – don't worry. Like anything else, it's a muscle you build over time. Here's how to start:

- **Catch the critic.** Become aware of when your thoughts take a negative turn. Are you catastrophising? Making assumptions? Comparing unfairly?
- **Challenge it.** Ask: *is this thought helpful? Is it true? Would I say this to someone I love?* If not, it has no place in your inner dialogue.

- **Change the language.** Flip the script. Swap 'I always mess this up' with 'I'm still learning how to do this well.'
- **Use voice notes or mirror work.** Yes, it can feel awkward. But saying your affirmations out loud – into your phone, or directly to yourself in the mirror – makes them more powerful. You hear them differently. You *feel* them differently.
- **Anchor your words to movement.** Pair affirmations with action. Say, 'I am energised,' *and* go for a walk. Say, 'I am focused,' and then sit down to work. The body remembers what you pair with words.

Speak to yourself like someone you love

Here's a simple truth: if your inner voice isn't kind, you won't believe the rest of the world when it is kind.

So often we wait for external validation to feel good about ourselves. But it has to start inside. You can't rely on applause to silence doubt. That's your job. Your inner voice isn't just commentary – it's direction. It tells your mind and body how to respond to challenge, to uncertainty, to growth.

So let it be encouraging. Let it be honest. Let it be on your side.

Because the most powerful thing you'll ever affirm isn't what you want. It's who you're becoming on the way to getting it.

Using the Five Principles to structure your actions

In earlier chapters, we've repeatedly returned to the Five Principles: career, entrepreneurship, family and relationships, self and health. These principles are not just themes for introspection – they're practical filters for planning.

Let's walk through an example using the affirmation: 'I am living a fulfilled and balanced life.'

Now, break that down by principle:

- **Career** Have you taken steps towards growth or progression? Are you working on that certification? Have you applied for the job you really want? Had the conversation about that raise?
- **Entrepreneurship** Are you reinvesting in your business? Have you identified your most profitable service? Are your processes aligned with your income goals?
- **Family and relationships** Have you scheduled quality time this week? Reached out to a loved one? Set boundaries to protect your energy and time?
- **Self** Have you checked in with yourself emotionally? Made space for joy, hobbies or solitude? Is your internal self-talk encouraging or critical?
- **Health** Are you moving your body? Drinking water? Getting enough sleep? Have you booked that long-overdue health check?

Once you map your affirmation against these principles, you'll quickly see where your actions are aligned – and where they're not. That's where the work begins. That's where the transformation lives.

Your turn: Create your affirmation plan

Here's a simple but effective way to get started:

1 Write down three affirmations you believe (or want to believe) about yourself. Start each with 'I am ...' or 'I create ...'
2 For each affirmation, write one to three supporting actions you can take this week. Make them specific. Make them time-bound.
3 Schedule those actions into your week. Put them in your calendar like you would a meeting.
4 At the end of the week, reflect on how it went. Did you act in alignment with your affirmations?
5 If yes, celebrate it. If no, adjust and recommit.

This isn't about perfection – it's about *progress with purpose.*

Because manifestation doesn't happen when you say the words. It happens when you live like they're already true.

Reflection and integration – making it stick

You've made it to the end of the chapter – and if you've been reading with an open mind, you'll have already started to feel the shift. Not because I've said anything revolutionary, but because *you've given yourself permission* to reframe what you think about affirmations, mindset and self-talk.

This is the moment where the reading stops and the *integration* begins. And that's really what manifested action is about: living the work.

You don't need to overhaul your life overnight. You don't need a new journal, a new routine or a new identity to get started. You just need to *begin where you are*, with what you've got, and move forward with more intention than before.

Because here's the truth I want to leave you with.

Affirmations are not promises. They are possibilities. And you bring them to life – not with your lips alone, but with your actions, your habits and your mindset.

Reflection exercise: Your affirmation in action

Take a moment to revisit the affirmation you chose earlier, or choose a new one now.

Write it down clearly: 'I am . . .'

_____

_____

Now, complete this process to make it real:

1 **Why this affirmation?**

_____

_____

2 **What does it represent? Why does it matter to you now?**

_____

_____

3 **What has your past shown you about this affirmation?**

_____

_____

4 **Where have you lived this truth before? Where have you struggled with it?**

_____

_____

5 **What actions in your present support (or sabotage) it?**

_____

_____

6 **Be honest. Are you behaving like someone who believes this about themselves?**

_____

_____

7 **What would it look like to live this affirmation this week?**

_____

_____

8 **List three small, specific steps that would align with this truth.**

• _____

• _____

• _____

9 **How will you reinforce it daily?**

_____

_____

_____

10 **Will you write it on your mirror? Say it aloud in the car? Set a calendar reminder?**

_____

_____

Setting the stage for success

Affirmation + Action = Alignment

If you take nothing else from this chapter, let it be this:

- You can absolutely desire more for your life.
- You can want financial freedom, success, impact, love, joy and peace.
- You can speak it, write it and believe it.
- But if you want it to *stick*, you must do the work.
- You must act as though your future self is already real – and, every day, inch closer towards them.

You don't have to believe it all at once. You just have to believe it enough to begin. And then do it again. And again. And again.

That's how you move from wishful words to a witnessed reality.

CHAPTER ELEVEN
No Time for Excuses, Time to Take Action

The final push

Life gets busy. The days blur into each other, and before you know it, another week, another month, another year has passed, and those dreams you've been carrying still live only in your head. It's easy to romanticise a better life, to call that moment of escape *manifestation*. But if this book has taught you anything, we hope it's this:

Manifestation without action is not enough.

If you want to build a life you love – across *all* Five Principles: career, entrepreneurship, family and relationships, self and health – you need more than vision. More than Pinterest boards, journaling prompts or waiting for a 'sign'. You need to plan *and* execute. Dream *and* do. Manifest *and* move.

Let us be transparent with you. We're manifesting another best-seller. Boldly, intentionally and unapologetically. But that would have been impossible if we hadn't sat down – day after day – and actually written this book. And it wouldn't be happening at all if *you* weren't here, reading it, engaging with it and investing in your own growth.

So thank you. Your decision to buy this book, to open it, to read it through – *that was your first act of commitment*. But now, here we are. The final push. The moment just before a new reality is birthed.

And we have to ask you: what action will you take to close the gap between vision and reality? Because that's where your power lives. In the choice you make next.

In the phone call you place.
In the application you submit.
In the habit you change.
In the 'yes' you finally say – or the 'no' you've been avoiding.

By now, if you've truly engaged with each chapter and completed the reflections, you should have a roadmap. A blueprint that suits the future *you* want – not one dictated by others, or social media trends or old limitations, but one built on clarity, confidence and purpose.

So now we ask: what will you do about it?

Because this isn't the end. It's the beginning of the life you said you wanted.

Let's be honest – the reality of delay and excuses

Let's have a real moment here – just us and you.

You've come this far. You've invested your time and energy into reading a book that wasn't just a motivational boost or quick fix but a framework. A strategy. A mindset shift. This wasn't supposed to be just another feel-good read to leave on the shelf. This isn't a January resolution you half-commit to before forgetting what your goal was by spring.

This is a blueprint for how you live the rest of your life.

So the question now is: **how badly do you actually want it?**

Because if we're being honest – and we are – for most people it is dangerously easy to get stuck in the *thinking* phase. Dreaming. Planning. Making lists. Rewriting them. Waiting for permission. Hoping for the right time. And telling themselves they're 'manifesting' when, actually, they're just *avoiding*.

And listen, we say that with love, not judgement. We've both been there.

We know the script because we've heard it hundreds of times from people with incredible potential:

- 'I'm just waiting for the right time.'
- 'I need to get everything perfect before I launch.'
- 'I've been meaning to start, but life is just hectic right now.'

We're going to say something that might feel uncomfortable, but we say it with love: **if you're waiting for perfect, you're waiting for never.**

There will always be something else. A reason to delay. A new fear, a fresh distraction, a louder opinion. But nothing changes unless *you* decide that the excuses no longer run the show.

And we're not judging – we've been there.

I (Byron) remember being in my early twenties, sitting on a goldmine of ideas. I wasn't waiting for someone to 'see my potential', but I was definitely caught up in the belief that dreaming big was enough. Spoiler: it's not. *Dreaming isn't a strategy.* I had to get moving – messy, imperfect, sometimes uncomfortable movement. That's when things shifted.

But let's rewind for a moment. I grew up on a council estate in a single-parent home, with a sister who contracted meningitis and became a quadruple amputee. Manifesting a better life for myself and my family wasn't some abstract vision-board idea. It was *urgent*. It was *survival*. It meant starting early – selling sweets at school, CDs and cars in college, moving into the property business, and eventually launching my first business.

Did I get everything right? Not even close. But I started. And I learned. And I got better. I don't believe the world – or the universe – rewards perfection. **It rewards movement. It rewards resilience. It rewards those who take that first shaky step.**

I (Bianca) know the power of fear. I also know the power of stepping through it. One of my biggest 'do it scared' moments came when I decided to go on BBC's *The Apprentice*. Millions of people watching. One of the biggest shows in the country at the time. There was every chance I'd get fired early. There was every chance I'd say or do something that would harm my personal brand. And statistically? It was more likely I'd be fired than make it to the final.

Every week on that show was a baptism of fire – people on social media commenting on my race, my appearance, my choices, my tone of voice. And yet, I kept going. I believed in myself, even when it would have been easier to shrink. Why? Because I live by what I call my 'deathbed philosophy' – when I look back at my life, I want to say, 'I tried,' not, 'What if?'

So . . . *what if you did the same?*

And let's not sugar-coat it – every business we've ever built together has been a risk. Every launch, every pitch, every stage we've stepped on to has come with uncertainty, pressure and a very real chance of failing. If you think it's easy to keep putting yourself out there, you don't yet understand the reality of entrepreneurship, or of *life at any level worth reaching.*

But you don't need to be on TV. You don't need to have grown up on an estate or built a business. You just need to decide that **your excuses no longer get to run the show**.

You've read the reflections. You've seen the steps. Now it's time to be radically honest with yourself:

- Do you want the promotion?
- Do you want the side hustle?
- Do you want to transform your finances, relationships or lifestyle?

Then stop waiting for clarity to fall into your lap. **Clarity comes through action. Confidence comes through action. Success comes through consistent, aligned action.**

You don't have to get it right. You just have to get it going.

So let us ask you again, with love and directness:

Are you treating your dreams like a priority or a hobby?

This is the moment where you get to be radically honest with yourself. No performative positivity. No pretending. Just the truth.

- Do you actually want the business?
- Do you truly want the career change?
- Do you deeply desire the freedom, the love, the legacy?
- And if you do – *what are you willing to sacrifice, change or do differently to get there?*

Because if you treat this like just another 'thing to read', you'll go back to the same patterns. But if you treat this like what it was designed to be – a strategy – you could literally change the course of your entire life.

This is your 'line in the sand' moment.

Your opportunity to move from intention to initiation.

No more waiting. No more watching others live out the dream while you hold back.

It's your turn.

The case for urgency

Let's cut to the chase: *someday* is a fantasy.

There is no perfect time. There is only *now*, and what you choose to do with it.

We often hear people say, 'I'll start when I have more time,' or, 'I just need to get through this month,' or, 'Next year is my year.' And while they're saying that, someone else is already doing it. Someone with less time, fewer resources, and just as much fear is out there *starting*. Imperfectly. Quietly. Courageously.

Here's a truth we've seen over and over again in our careers as entrepreneurs, mentors and educators:

It's rarely the most talented person who wins. It's the person who moves.

Because time is not just passing – it's compounding. Every moment you delay taking action is a moment you could have been learning, growing, earning, connecting and becoming. Every 'I'll do it later' is a silent surrender to comfort and avoidance.

And look – we get it.

We're not here to add pressure for the sake of it. Life is busy. Some days feel like a marathon with no medal in sight. Especially if you're juggling a job, a family, a business, your health – or all of the above.

But, if not now, when?

Waiting for things to calm down before you pursue your dream is like waiting for silence in a house full of toddlers. **There's always going to be something.**

And so the urgency we're talking about isn't panic. It's not impulsivity. It's *intentional movement*. It's the decision to honour your vision by doing one small thing *today* that brings you closer to the life you've been talking about.

That's the real meaning of manifested action. Not a leap off a cliff. Not a dramatic overnight transformation. Just a step.

One step forward.
One email sent.
One hour focused.
One call made.
One decision, finally taken.

That's what creates the ripple. That's what builds the shift. That's what takes you from the 'I wish' to the 'I did'.

So the question isn't: 'Do you have time?' The question is:

Will you make time for what matters?

Because the truth is, if you don't make time for your dreams, life will make time for your regrets.

MANIFESTED ACTION IN MOTION

You've made it to the final stretch. You've done the thinking, the reflecting, the realising. And now – this is where the *real* work begins.

Because manifested action isn't a one-off. It's not a launch. It's not a Monday motivation post or a January detox plan. It's not something you try out for a few weeks and then forget when life gets busy again.

Manifested action is a way of living. A decision you make every day to align your choices with your vision.

That means keeping your goals in plain sight, not tucked away in a notebook you'll never open again. It means returning to the hard questions, the ones that made you uncomfortable. It means having the courage to pivot when something no longer serves you – and the discipline to persist when things get tough.

It's not about doing everything at once. It's about doing *something* consistently.

Let's say that again, because it's everything:

Manifested action is not about doing everything. It's about doing something – consistently.

We've worked with thousands of people – entrepreneurs, professionals, parents, creatives – people with wildly different backgrounds and wildly powerful dreams. And the ones who change their lives? They're not always the ones with the most time, money or talent.

They're the ones who *keep showing up.*

Even when it's hard. Even when the result doesn't come immediately. Even when it feels like nobody is watching.

They've built momentum, one step at a time. They've applied what they've learned. They've made movement a non-negotiable part of their identity.

And now it's your turn.

Here's what we want you to take from this section:

- Don't just *know* what to do. *Do it.*
- Don't wait until you 'feel ready'. Ready is a myth.
- Don't aim for perfect. Aim for progress.
- Don't think your first action has to be huge. It just has to be honest. Maybe your first step is . . .
  - having a conversation you've been avoiding
  - setting a boundary
  - launching that website
  - submitting the application

- ○ raising your prices
- ○ asking for help
- ○ writing the first paragraph
- ● Whatever it is – do it. **Today, not tomorrow.**

Because once you start, everything shifts. Your confidence grows. Your belief deepens. The world responds differently when you begin to act like you believe in yourself.

You've spent the last ten chapters learning how to dream bigger, think smarter and act stronger.

Now it's time to **live it**.

Take action

This is your call to stop rereading and start *rewriting* – your habits, your results, your story.

But before you do, we want to return to something that has been a thread throughout this book: the Five Principles of Manifested Action. These aren't just categories – they're the foundations of a meaningful, balanced, abundant life. They're where your dreams live and where your reality is built.

So, as you move into action, here's what we want you to remember across each principle:

1. CAREER

You don't need to wait for someone to 'tap you on the shoulder' or open a door. You are more than qualified to carve your own space. Whether you're seeking promotion, pivoting industries or reigniting passion in your current role, decide what you want and back yourself by learning, showing up, speaking up and stretching further than you have before.

Take the lead in your career journey. *You are not a passenger.*

2. ENTREPRENEURSHIP

If you've got a business idea, the time to start is not one day. It's day one. Whether you're scaling an existing business or starting from scratch, understand this: no one is coming to rescue your dream. Be bold. Test, learn, launch, fail, recover. Ask for help. Find your market. Know your numbers.

Your business becomes real the day you treat it like it already is.

3. FAMILY AND RELATIONSHIPS

Whether you're navigating partnership, parenting, friendships or chosen family – this principle demands intention. Love is not passive. Connection is not automatic. Show up for your people. Ask for what you need. Offer what you can. Learn to balance giving and protecting your energy.

Your legacy isn't just what you build – it's who you build it with.

4. SELF

Stop making yourself the lowest priority. The version of you who achieves your goals? They need sleep, peace, joy, focus and fire. They need space to breathe. Invest in therapy. Take the solo trip. Build boundaries. Set your standards higher. Choose joy on purpose.

Manifestation without self-awareness is like driving without a map.

5. HEALTH

This principle underpins them all. Without physical vitality and mental clarity, the journey becomes ten times harder. Move your body. Feed it well. Protect your mental health like a priceless resource – because it is.

Your body and mind are the vehicle of your purpose. Treat them accordingly.

Manifested action isn't about perfection in every area. It's about alignment. It's about recognising that your vision for your life deserves your daily investment.

Every choice you make today – how you speak to yourself, what you prioritise, who you surround yourself with – is either building that life or postponing it.

You have everything you need to begin.

Now act like it.

A final affirmation from Bianca and Byron

We've written this book not just as authors, not just as entrepreneurs, but as two people who have dared – again and again – to believe in something bigger.

And now we pass that belief on to you.

We don't know the exact goal you're holding. We don't know how long you've been carrying it. But we know this: you would not have the vision if you didn't also have the ability to bring it to life.

You don't need to be perfect. You don't need to have it all figured out.

You don't need to move mountains.

You just need to move – forward.

We've coached people with no budget, no business experience and no formal qualifications who went on to build six- and seven-figure businesses, write books, take the stage, change industries, and transform their family's future.

And we've seen people with all the 'right' ingredients – education, funding, connections – who stayed exactly where they were. Not because they couldn't do more . . . but because they didn't *start*.

So let's be clear: belief is a muscle. The more you use it, the stronger it gets. But belief without movement? That's just noise. Belief paired with action? That's momentum. That's what changes everything.

Whether your journey begins with a whispered prayer, a Post-it note on your mirror, a late-night idea, or a leap of faith – start now.

Make the call.

Write the plan.

Book the class.

Pitch the idea.

Change the habit.

Say the affirmation.

Take the damn step.

The only thing between where you are and where you want to be . . . is what you choose to do next.

We believe in you.

Now it's time for you to believe in you.

Closing words . . . and thank you!

If you've made it to this point, know this: we don't take it lightly.

Thank you for your time.

Thank you for your belief in what we stand for.

And most of all, thank you for your commitment to yourself.

From our first book, *Self Made*, to *The Business Survival Kit*, *Rich Forever* and now *Manifested Action*, this has never been about just words on a page. It's been about transformation. About progress. About turning dreams into plans, and plans into real, tangible success.

To every client, mentee, student, reader and supporter who has joined us at a training session, signed up to a course, attended our academies, read our books, watched a webinar, or engaged with us on socials, **you are the embodiment of manifested action**. You've proven that belief paired with bold movement creates real change.

We are truly honoured that you manifested *us* into your world – as mentors, coaches, consultants and champions. Whether we've worked together closely or from a distance, you are part of our community, and your wins matter to us.

So let's keep the momentum going.

When you take action on what you've learned, share it with us. Use the hashtag **#ManifestedAction** to show the world your journey – and tag us so we can celebrate every milestone right alongside you.

Instagram: @biancamillerofficial + @mrbselfmade

LinkedIn: Bianca Miller-Cole + Dr Byron Cole

And if this book has lit a fire in you, don't keep it to yourself.

Buy it for someone you love.

Share it with your team.

Loan it to your inner circle.

Success is so much sweeter when shared.

So take the people you care about on this journey with you.

Because action is exponentially more powerful when shared by a community.

Thank you for choosing to walk this path with us.

Thank you for believing in better — for yourself and for others.

And thank you for being part of a world where we dream *and* do.

With admiration, belief and commitment to your success,
Bianca and Byron

Appendix
Reflection and Manifested Action Plan

This isn't just a book you've read. It's a manual for the life you've said you want.

And now, it's time to put pen to paper.

We want you to take a moment. Carve out a quiet space. And answer these questions honestly, without rushing. This is your opportunity to capture the clarity that's now at your fingertips.

STEP 1: Grounding your vision

1 **What is the life I am actively working towards? (Think about your career, business, family, personal growth, health. Be specific.)**

Write here:

_____

_____

_____

_____

_____

2 **Why is this important to me? (What are the values behind this vision? What's at stake if I don't pursue it?)**

Write here:

_____

_____

_____

_____

STEP 2: Confronting what's been holding you back

3 **What excuses have I been making that I need to release? (Where have I delayed, avoided or self-sabotaged?)**

Write here:

_____

_____

_____

_____

4 **What fears or doubts still linger, and how can I reframe them into action?**

Write here:

_____

_____

_____

_____

_____

STEP 3: *Action that aligns*

5 **What are three specific goals I want to manifest in the next 6–12 months? (Be bold, detailed and truthful. No playing small.)**

Goal 1: _____

Goal 2: _____

Goal 3: _____

6 **What is ONE action I will take in the next 48 hours to start the momentum? (Not a big leap – just a first aligned step.)**

Write here:

_____

_____

_____

_____

_____

STEP 4: *Building my support and accountability*

7 **Who do I need in my life right now to support my vision? (Think: mentors, friends, partners, professionals. Use Bianca's Personal Board Framework in Chapter 7 if needed.)**

Write here:

_____

_____

_____

_____

_____

8 **How will I remain accountable to myself and others? (What systems, routines or check-ins will keep you on track?)**

Write here:

_____

_____

_____

_____

STEP 5: *Declaring it out loud*

9 **My Manifested Action affirmation. Write your own powerful, personal affirmation that ties it all together.**

'I am . . .'
'I believe . . .'
'I act . . .'
'I become . . .'

Write here:

_____

_____

_____

_____

_____

Final words

You're not starting from scratch. You're starting from *now*.
From knowledge. From clarity. From belief. From action.
 Revisit this plan weekly. Add to it. Evolve it.
 But whatever you do, don't let it gather dust.
 Your future is waiting. Your actions will bring it home.

Notes

Chapter 1

1 Proverbs 23:7, The Bible, King James Version. Public domain.
2 Philippians 4:13, The Holy Bible, New International Version (2011).
3 Proverbs 21:5, The Holy Bible, New International Version (2011).
4 The Qur'an, trans. M. A. S. Abdel Haleem (Oxford: Oxford University Press, 2004).
5 *Bhagavad Gita: As It Is*, trans. A. C. Bhaktivedanta Swami Prabhupada (Alachua, FL: The Bhaktivedanta Book Trust, 1983).

Chapter 2

1 Spice Girls, 'Wannabe', *Spice* (UK: Virgin Records, 1996).

Chapter 5

1 Clare O'Connor (@Clare_OC), '@WhitWolfeHerd gave all 700ish of us a paid week off . . .', Twitter, unknown date. Cited in Lucia Binding, 'Dating app Bumble closes for a week to let staff tackle "collective burnout"', *Sky News*, 22 June 2021, https://news.sky.com/story/dating-app-bumble-closes-for-a-week-to-let-staff-tackle-collective-burnout-12338285

Chapter 6

1 Samad Esmaeilzadeh, Susanne Kumpulainen and Arto J. Pesola, 'Strength-cognitive training: A systemic review in adults and older adults, and guidelines to promote "strength exergaming" innovations', *Frontiers in Psychology,* 13 (2022), https://doi.org/10.3389/fpsyg.2022.855703
2 Francesca Barigozzi, Pietro Biroli, Chiara Monfardini, Natalia Montinari, Elena Pisanelli and Sveva Vitellozzi, 'Beyond time: Unveiling the invisible

burden of mental load', IZA Discussion Paper No. 17912 (Bonn: IZA – Institute of Labor Economics, 2025).

3 Tiffany Dufu, *Drop the Ball: Achieving More by Doing Less* (New York: Flatiron Books, 2017).

Chapter 7

1 Billy Gene, keynote speech, EMC (Entrepreneurs Marketing Conference), London, 2 December 2022.

2 Sheryl Sandberg, *Lean In: Women, Work, and the Will to Lead* (London: WH Allen, 2015).

3 Bob Burg and John D. Mann, *The Go-Giver: A Little Story about a Powerful Business Idea* (New York: Portfolio, 2007).

4 Luke 6:38, The Holy Bible, New International Version (2011).

Chapter 8

1 Rachel Rodgers, *We Should All be Millionaires: A Woman's Guide to Earning More, Building Wealth, and Gaining Economic Power* (New York: HarperCollins Leadership, 2022).

2 Guo Feng, Xiaxia Xu and Jiawei Lei, 'Tracking perceived stress, anxiety, and depression in daily life: A double-downward spiral process', *Frontiers in Psychology,* 14 (2023), https://doi.org/10.3389/fpsyg.2023.1114332

Chapter 9

1 'legacy, n.', *Merriam Webster,* https://www.merriam-webster.com/dictionary/legacy

Chapter 10

1 John David Creswell, James K. Bursley and Ajay B. Satpute, 'Neural reactivation links unconscious thought to decision-making performance', *Social Cognitive and Affective Neuroscience,* 8:8 (2013), 863–9, https://doi.org/10.1093/scan/nst004

2 David Tod, James Hardy and Emily J. Oliver, 'Effects of self-talk: A systematic review', *Journal of Sport and Exercise Psychology,* 33:5 (2011), 666–87, https://doi.org/10.1123/jsep.33.5.666

Also by Bianca Miller-Cole and Dr Byron Cole

Rich Forever: What They Didn't Teach You about Money, Finance and Investments in School

We all want financial freedom. But we also know just how much pressure the subject of money exerts on us, and many of us feel our personal finances are out of control. But that's not surprising – after all, no one ever explained how to manage money properly – or if they did, we didn't listen.

If a head-in-the-sand approach to personal finance ever worked, it doesn't now. Not only do we openly worry about the state of our finances and the cost of living, we increasingly yearn for the kind of financial independence which will enable us to do our own thing and live life to the full. This paradox is right at the heart of everything we do, and a solution is needed.

You will learn how to be rich forever – rich in time, rich in freedom, rich in opportunity. So although this book is about money, from two authors who have astonishing rags-to-riches business stories, it is a self-help book in every way – a handbook to transforming the way you think and feel about a subject that exerts a grip on almost everything we do. This book will loosen the grip, and free you to grow.

Hardback ISBN: 978 1 399 80759 3
Ebook ISBN: 978 1 399 80761 6
Audio ISBN: 978 1 399 80760 9

For more information, please visit www.johnmurraypress.co.uk

RAISING READERS
Books Build Bright Futures

Dear Reader,

We'd love your attention for one more page to tell you about the crisis in children's reading, and what we can all do.

Studies have shown that reading for fun is the **single biggest predictor of a child's future life chances** – more than family circumstance, parents' educational background or income. It improves academic results, mental health, wealth, communication skills, ambition and happiness.[1]

The number of children reading for fun is in rapid decline. Young people have a lot of competition for their time. In 2024, 1 in 10 children and young people in the UK aged 5 to 18 did not own a single book at home.[2]

Hachette works extensively with schools, libraries and literacy charities, but here are some ways we can all raise more readers:

- Reading to children for just 10 minutes a day makes a difference
- Don't give up if children aren't regular readers – there will be books for them!
- Visit bookshops and libraries to get recommendations
- Encourage them to listen to audiobooks
- Support school libraries
- Give books as gifts

There's a lot more information about how to encourage children to read on our website: **www.RaisingReaders.co.uk**

Thank you for reading.

---

[1] OECD, '21st-Century Readers: Developing Literacy Skills in a Digital World', 2021, https://www.oecd.org/en/publications/21st-century-readers_a83d84cb-en.html

[2] National Literacy Trust, 'Book Ownership in 2024', November 2024, https://literacytrust.org.uk/research-services/research-reports/book-ownership-in-2024